GN
495.8
.D39
1993

BARBARIC OTHERS

D1026867

Merryl Wyn Davies, writer and television producer, is the author of *Knowing One Another: Shaping an Islamic Anthropology* (1988) and co-author of *Distorted Imagination: Lessons from the Rushdie Affair* (1990). Forever Welsh, she lives and works in Kuala Lumpur, Malaysia.

Ashis Nandy is one of the most respected and influential writers of India. Author of *Alternative Sciences* (1980), *The Intimate Enemy* (1983), *Traditions, Tyranny and Utopias* (1987), *Tao of Cricket* (1990) and other works, he is a Senior Fellow at the Centre for the Study of Developing Societies, Delhi.

Ziauddin Sardar, writer, broadcaster and cultural critic, is one of the most noted intellectuals of the Muslim world. His numerous books include *The Future of Muslim Civilization* (1979), *Islamic Futures: The Shape of Ideas to Come* (1985), *Information and the Muslim World* (1988), *Explorations in Islamic Science* (1989) and, as co-author, *Distorted Imagination: Lessons from the Rushdie Affair* (1990). Of Pakistani origin, he lives and works in London.

Media Center (Library)
Elizabethtown Community College
Elizabethtown, KY 42701

BARBARIC OTHERS

A Manifesto on Western Racism

**Merryl Wyn Davies, Ashis Nandy
and Ziauddin Sardar**

Pluto Press

LONDON / BOULDER, COLORADO

First published 1993 by Pluto Press
345 Archway Road, London N6 5AA
and 5500 Central Avenue
Boulder, Colorado 80301, USA

Copyright © Merryl Wyn Davies, Ashis Nandy, and
Ziauddin Sardar, 1993.

The right of Merryl Wyn Davies, Ashis Nandy, and
Ziauddin Sardar to be identified as authors of this work
has been asserted by them in accordance with the
Copyright, Designs and Patents Act, 1988.

British Library Cataloguing in Publication Data
A catalogue record for this book is available from
the British Library

ISBN 0 7453 0742 6 hb
ISBN 0 7453 0743 4 pb

Library of Congress Cataloging in Publication Data
Applied for.

Designed and produced for Pluto Press by
Chase Production Services, Chipping Norton, OX7 5QR

Printed in the EC by TJ Press

CONTENTS

CONTENTS

Introduction

FIVE HUNDRED YEARS AGO, in 1492, Christopher Columbus set sail across the Atlantic in search of a new route to 'the Indies'. The historic voyage inaugurated a startling new epoch for the Europe that Columbus represented, ushered in an age of unparalleled repression for the diverse peoples living across the ocean and beyond.

The unprecedented encounter that lay in wait at the end of that journey signally failed to become a new departure in Europe's relations with Other People. The Americas would be called a New World. This world was a natural environment new to European experience, populated by cultures wholly new to the citizens of Christian Europe. Yet it was the ideas and reflexes of the old world that crossed the Atlantic with Columbus and settled the fate of the enterprise of the Indies.

For centuries Europe had nurtured an anxiety-ridden perception about Other People, those beyond its actual touch and reach, and about the natural world. Woven in monstrous and phantasmagoric detail, based primarily on fears, fantasies and demons inhabiting the Western mind from Herodotus to Pliny, and from St Augustine to Columbus, this perception had become an integral part of Europe's self-identity. The antique convention found new life in the new continent Europe was meeting for the first time.

One might think that the surprising newness of the experiences launched in 1492 could have exposed the lie at the heart of Europe's self-delusion, yet events prove this to

be a fanciful dream. It was through old and familiar ideas
that the New World was made known to Europe. The
voyages that commenced in 1492 ended up endorsing and
further legitimising a great lie. Instead of an encounter,
Columbus's voyage inaugurated a sundering of Europe
from Other People, a rupture that has yet to be healed and
overcome.

The events of 1492 are, in a profound sense, a Greek
tragedy. They were a function of the intellectual debt
Europe owes to Greek thought. And, like a classical Greek
tragedy, their consequences have been inexorable, full of
human suffering and mired in blood. The results have been
global in extent and continue to disable the best hopes of
people everywhere for better relations among all of
mankind and with the natural world we share. A mere 29
years separate Columbus's first voyage and Magellan's
circumnavigation of the globe. Today we all inhabit the
aftermath of that intense burst of globalisation. We are all
fellow travellers in the Columbian wake.

The Dutch geographer and map maker Gerhardus
Mercator compiled the new information that so suddenly
became available about the world. He gave us the visual
image of an Atlantic-centred world as Columbus's most
potent legacy. It was Mercator, too, who said that history is
the eye of the world, its *oculus mundi*. The historic events of
1492 made possible an even greater deformation in the eye
of the West, and the induction of a cancerous and fatal
stage in the unfolding of its soul. Of course, we have been
affected as well, for in turn we too have been unable to
resist the equally self-destructive claims of the Columbus
within. Thus we find ourselves today trapped in a 'history'
that moves in ever-decreasing, ever-constricting, concentric

circles. At the epicentre of this tornado is the lie, the great lie, about the nature of the West and about the nature of the Others, about Us and Them and the relationship of all to nature: what it ought to be, what it has tragically become.

To many, this wholly new and unconventional reading of the European past will appear audacious and troubling. We see in it instead the germ of a manifesto, a call to break out of a history that has managed, with some depressing success, not only to strip all not-Western people of their humanity and identify but to enslave the West itself, and that threatens to deprive both the West and the not-West of the creative, liberating means to address the pressing issues of today, including the survival of planet Earth.

We are still living out the history of 1492. In that year a real encounter across cultures was waylaid by the blinded eye of history. The possibilities that were overlooked and unseen 500 years ago must re-emerge as humanity's project over the next 500 years.

1 US

CHRISTOPHER COLUMBUS was a man on the make, an adventurer in search of advancement in the most conventional manner of his time. The second half of the fifteenth century was a time of economic expansion throughout Europe. The great depopulation of the previous century caused by the plague (the 'Black Death') had left plenty of scope and space for new men on the rise in all European societies.

The prosperity of the city of Columbus's birth, Genoa, was founded on its trading links with the Muslim world, source of many of the necessities and practically all of the luxuries of European life, and on bulk trade with the Atlantic fringes of Europe. Genoan merchants formed thriving communities throughout the Iberian peninsula and operated in Britain, Holland and France. Trading and seafaring were an inseparable part of the Genoan way of life. The dispersed communities of compatriots provided a ready and obvious support system for any young man who, in time-honoured local fashion, went to sea to make his fortune.

Voyages into Atlantic waters were licensed by monarchs, since royal warrant was the only means by which to protect and lay secure claim to whatever marketable resource one might acquire. The warrant protected not merely the right of exploitation but also one's entry into the regulated system of trade that operated throughout Europe. Spain, Portugal and England, before whose monarchs Columbus sought to advance his 'enterprise of the Indies', all had a growing interest in their Atlantic waters. In fact, a lively rivalry existed between them for new Atlantic possessions.

Both Portugal and Spain had a clear motive behind their interest in Atlantic exploration. Both countries were culturally influenced and enriched by the Muslim world. Indeed, Muslims had been in Spain for over 800 years, and both Spain and Portugal were unique in Europe for being genuinely plural societies, a history they were now determined to expunge. Their entry as nations onto the European stage was the result of the *reconquista*, the rolling back of Muslim control of their territory. Portugal had completed the process in 1249, while Spain achieved its final victory over Granada in January 1492, just three months before the royal warrant for Columbus's first voyage was granted. It is hardly surprising, then, that their prime interest in the Atlantic was to make further inroads into Muslim dominance.

The Iberian powers were motivated by two aspects of Muslim supremacy that were of particular economic importance. The Muslim Levant dominated trade with the Indies from which came the spices and luxuries that made European life palatable and tolerable. To obtain these goods, whose trade within Europe was dominated by the merchants of Venice and Genoa, there was an acute need for gold. The gold that underwrote European currencies and trade throughout the Middle Ages came across the Sahara from the riverine goldfields of West Africa to Morocco, and thence entered European circulation before passing out again into the Muslim realms further east. As a consequence, the economic trends of the medieval world placed Europe at a disadvantage in that it was a net contributor to the wealth of the Muslim world.

The first expansion beyond Europe's own boundaries was made by the Portuguese, who intended to secure control of the trans-Saharan gold routes. They captured Ceuta, in North Africa, in 1415, but there was no gold to be discovered in Morocco itself, nor was one foothold sufficient to annex the gold trade. It is probable that Portugal's contact with the Maghrib provided it with useful information about the coast and interior of Africa and triggered the idea of striking nearer to the source of the gold trade, thereby outflanking the long-established overland trade network by sea. The Portuguese voyages that edged their way down the coast of Africa were all private ventures, quite often outright piracy, legitimised by a grander chivalric, and hence inevitably crusading, motif. Malyn Newitt (1986) argues that this was the reality behind the hagiography of that other paragon of the 'age of discovery', Prince Henry the Navigator, of Portugal.

Thus the overturning of Muslim dominance in European affairs was a persistent medieval European concept that could be called upon to legitimise any kind of action. It already had an Atlantic content and meaning before Columbus entered the fray. The Portuguese had a fort at Mina on the West African coast supplying gold and slaves. Both Portugal and Spain had established colonies on the Atlantic islands of the Azores, the Canaries and Cape Verde. The settlers who were sent to these islands were engaged in subduing the native population and developing their economic potential for national purposes. The most lucrative product of the islands was sugar. Columbus's early career included merchant ventures to the Canaries, where he married the daughter of a leading settler.

Ferdinand and Isabella, rulers of the united crowns of Aragon and Castile, found themselves lagging behind in the acquisition of new Atlantic territory. And they needed some other springboard from which to leapfrog the established pattern of Portuguese plans to reach the riches of the Indies. For all of Europe 'the Indies' was a vague term. It comprised both the underbelly of Muslim Africa and what lay beyond Muslim lands. In a sense, the Indies were all that was beyond Europe. At the precise time Columbus was seeking patronage for his novel enterprise of the Indies in Portugal and then Spain the internal social, political and economic circumstances of these countries demanded new sources of finance. The need for gold only highlighted the well-attested fact that there was gold to be had out there in Atlantic waters.

No European country could relish more than Spain or Portugal, the prospect of ending the Muslim hold on trade with the Indies and Africa. Each had a consistent history of implacable hostility to the Muslim world, despite (perhaps because of) having been part of that world. No other country had greater motivation to explore the Atlantic for its own objectives. Both countries also had a conceptual and legal framework for such ventures in the form of a series of papal bulls that provided the context to European expansion and to Europe's relationship with the non-European world. Both countries had also internalised the only viewpoint that made sense, and that influenced all of Europe's cultural and intellectual products – the Crusade.

Medieval monarchs legitimated their activities in the international sphere through the procuring of papal bulls.

They then subcontracted the pursuit of their vision to their clients. It should occasion little surprise, therefore, that there was remarkable overlap of conception, language and ideas between the terms of appointment Columbus was at such pains to wrest from the Spanish monarchs on his own behalf and what the monarchs of Spain and Portugal sought from the Pope. The papal bull Dum Diversas of 1452, for instance, the earliest in the series of bulls granted to the Portuguese, defined the conceptual context of Iberia's Atlantic venture. It was similar in conception to the warrant granted by the Spanish Borgia Pope, Alexander VI, to Ferdinand and Isabella before Columbus set sail. Dum Diversas authorised the King of Portugal to attack, conquer and subdue 'Saracens', pagans and other unbelievers who were inimical to Christ; to capture their goods and their territories; to reduce their persons to perpetual slavery; and to transfer their lands and the properties to the King of Portugal and his successors. Despite the fact that the papacy itself was an increasingly weak institution in the second half of the fifteenth century, the bulls represented the quintessence of European understanding of the time, a function of its essential *oculus mundi*, its way of seeing the world.

If the papal bulls provided the geo-political context for the Atlantic quest, the psycho-political context was provided by the Crusade – a theme that had been nurtured within the consciousness of western Christendom since 1099. To the Europe of Columbus's day the Crusades were neither a dead heritage nor an undertaking belonging only to the past. When crusading no longer took Europe to the Levant it remained alive and well on the Iberian peninsula. Chaucer's 'very parfit gentil knight' is described in the *Canterbury Tales* as the very model of the ideals and activity of the Christian gentleman. His list of exploits includes service in crusading military campaigns in Spain.

As Dum Diversas and Chaucer make clear, any non-Christian people could be an appropriate target for crusading. Crusades could cover the peoples of the Atlantic islands and Africa as well as the campaigns against the 'pagans' of northern Europe, where Chaucer's knight also saw action. Portugal, and later Spain, extended the geographic scope of the Crusade to the Maghrib, just as it had previously been extended to a multiplicity of Muslim and even Byzantine areas around the Mediterranean. The crusading imperative gained new impetus in the European imagination with the fall of Constantinople to the Ottoman empire in 1453. The papal bull Romanus Pontifex, of 1455, specifically credits the Portuguese king with seeking to circumnavigate Africa in order to make contact with the Indies where, it was hoped, Prester John, a Christian monarch, would be found. Throughout the Middle Ages, Prester John figured in European literature and was deemed to reside on the other side of the Muslim lands, somewhere out east.

Together with this potential ally, the bull expected Portugal to prosecute the struggle against the 'Saracen' and other enemies of Christ. In the same year Spain responded to papal exhortation for a new Crusade against the Turk by renewing its internal *reconquista* against Granada, the last Muslim kingdom on the Iberian peninsula. The Spanish monarchs also made occasional attempts to support their campaigns at home by attacks on the Balearics and North Africa, though they gained no possessions in North Africa until the completion of the conquest of Melilla in 1497.

The British monarchs were not far behind. The charter granted by Henry VII to John Cabot and his sons in 1482 licensed the seafarers to occupy and set up the king's banners and ensigns 'in any town, city, castle, island or mainland whatsoever, newly found by them', anywhere in the 'eastern, western and northern sea', belonging to 'heathens and infidels, in whatsoever part of the world placed, which before this time were unknown to all Christians'. The charter empowered them 'to conquer, occupy and possess' all such places, the main conditions being that they would give to the king 'the fifth part of the whole capital gained' in every voyage of their enterprise.

Into this setting stepped Christopher Columbus, seaman and would-be entrepreneur. The scheme he devised was a novel one: to outflank the Portuguese initiative by sailing to the Indies westward across the Atlantic. Though in itself a new scheme, the overall conception was just another in a well-trodden pattern of contemporary enterprises with conventional aims and purposes. Only his plan of action, to get east by a western route, marked him out.

A great deal has been made of how little we know of Columbus's background and early life. It has remained a rich source of hagiographic speculation, for a larger-than-life figure sufficiently enigmatic to support contradictory interpretations. Yet the little that is known is more than sufficient to render Columbus, his career, ideas and aspirations wholly unremarkable in the context of his times. A practical apprenticeship at sea, in the waters of the Atlantic powers of Europe, was all that was necessary to set the scene for his career. The only addition required was a character trait that engendered a lively interest in the literary sources of his time. We know that, though not formally schooled, Columbus read the most representative of the conventional available literature. His regular reading consisted of *The Book of Marco Polo*, Pliny's *Historia Naturalis* and *The Travels of Sir John Mandeville*. But his favourite text was Pierre d'Ailly's *Imago Mundi*. Chapters from *Imago Mundi*, and the two cosmological and astrological treatises bound with it, were memorised, strung together in astounding patterns and regurgitated throughout Columbus's later life. But the 'Admiral', like so many Spanish sailors, was also aware of the genuinely scientific knowledge about the earth and the sea that Muslim scientists and scholars – who had measured the circumference of the earth some 700 years before Columbus was born – had passed on to Spain. His apprenticeship, his reading and the knowledge he had imbibed from Moorish culture are enough to explain why he conceived his particular grand design; how he sought to realise it; what he, and those who followed in his footsteps, as well as those more loosely connected with those activities, expected from his endeavour and its outcome.

Despite this, the legends have remained in circulation. What every schoolchild knows about 1492, for instance, is summed up in the lyrics of Jerome Kern: 'They all laughed at Christopher Columbus when he said the world was round.'

Popular folklore holds that Columbus's sailors feared they might fall off the edge of a flat earth if they sailed too far westwards across the Atlantic Ocean. This is all part of the potent myth of Columbus the discoverer, whose superior science and indomitable will alone saved the day, claimed an unknown continent, and unleashed the march of progress. It is a myth that is nothing but a triumphal piece of misinformation fabricated in the nineteenth century, most notably by the American writer Washington Irving. Like so much else in the history of Western self-image, the myth is an intelligent, knowledgeably fashioned work of ignorance.

Contrary to popular imagination, Columbus never had to convince anyone that the world was round. No self-respecting medieval scholar believed anything else. The medieval European view of the world was always round. It was a complex vision evolved to accommodate Biblical assertion and such learning from ancient Greece and Rome as was extant then in Europe. Thus the great Mappa Mundi of Hereford, made around 1280, is decidedly circular. It is both a representation of geograpical information and a map of ideas and ideology. It shows a land world surrounded by the encircling sea. The centre of the world is Jerusalem, the place where Christ walked on earth, placing the Christian vision at the heart of all understanding. Thrusting as near to Jerusalem and the centre as possible is Italy, dominated by Rome, the second ideological centre of the world.

This world was one of the concentric circles. The earth was understood to be a globe, a sphere, a perception that was a remnant of classical Greek and, later, Roman scholarship. While classical knowledge had waned in the Dark Ages, most seriously through the decline of Western European facility in Greek, the broad outline of what was known to the ancient world constituted the learning of the educated European of the Middle Ages. The sphere of the earth was believed to be divided into circular bands or zones. At the Equator was the torrid zone, believed impassable because of their great heat. Then there were two temperate zones, one in the northern hemisphere, the other in the southern – the antipodes. Lastly there were two polar zones of extreme cold which were uninhabitable.

It was also conventional wisdom that the antipodes, if they existed, were uninhabited. A delight in symmetry argued for the existence of a southern continent as counterweight to the great landmass of the known world. But the antipodes would have to be barren and unpopulated. This contention was confirmed by no less than an authority than St Augustine, who was a major force in reconciling classical knowledge within the biblical framework. The antipodes' lack of population was an important conceptual principle for the Middle Ages. To have believed otherwise would have necessitated a defiance of biblical exegesis by requiring a second incarnation of Christ. It was, however, an uncontroversial concept, since the ancient scholars had also believed in the impossibility of antipodean people.

The neatly zoned globe was graphically represented as a land world. Without a reliable measure of distance, the size of the known, travelled world was vastly expanded, with the extent of Europe around the Mediterranean, the Middle Sea, exaggerated. The distances comprising the further reaches of the habitable world were correspondingly shortened.

The fact that Columbus argued for a westward passage to the Indies does not mean that he was in some way enlightened. He was merely a dedicated believer in a small earth. He relied upon the retention of a classical error to support this grand design: basing his vision on the underestimation of the circumference of the globe by Ptolemy, he argued for the westward passage, thinking it to be the shortest route to the Indies. New copies of the works of Ptolemy were recovered and circulated in Western Europe in the early fifteenth century. Their popularity set an appropriate stage for Columbus's argument in favour of his endeavour. Columbus would claim to 'go where no man had gone before', but only as a reference to the plausible novelty of his route, not as a comment on his destination. The point at which he expected to arrive – and the place he maintained he had been – was the Indies. His insight was to combine latent possibilities within the available knowledge of his time.

An even better picture of standard medieval geographic thought is available in the Psalter map, another thirteenth-century work, now in the British Library. It is probably a miniature of the great map that once hung in Henry III's audience chamber at Whitehall. The Psalter map graphically represents the standard Ptolemaic argument for a land link between southern Africa and India. What is shown on this map is the Indian Ocean as an inland sea. Such a map gave further support to Columbus's novel argument. For what use was it for the Portuguese to inch their way down the coast of Africa when the route to the Indies could be blocked by the *terra incognita* of the land link with India?

From the eleventh to the fourteenth century – that is, during the high Middle Ages themselves – maps were no abstruse concern of the occasional scholar. They were

graphic encryptions of salient information. They were the
ideological representations of *oculus mundi*, a conception
of an integrated view of the earth and its origins as well
as man's place in that world and the diversity of mankind. Maps graphically displayed the integration of the
classical and the Biblical. Thus, the Psalter map records
what one would expect to find in the ambiguous spaces
of the Indies. Inset there is a series of 14 naked figures,
one with a dog's head, others of people with no head but
with their eyes and mouth on their torso, many recognis-
ably consuming human limbs. The monstrous peoples of
the Psalter map were known as the Plinian peoples from
their description in the *Historia Naturalis*, written by the
Roman Pliny the Elder.

Also shown on the Psalter map are the rivers of Eden,
located in the east, which appears at the top of the map
where the modern observer would expect to find the
North Pole. Just as we will find Columbus using the
conventional medieval notions of the Plinian people to
observe and identify the peoples of the lands he reached,
we also find that he identifies the delta of the Orinoco as
the outflow of the rivers of Paradise.

Both speculations confirmed his confidence in his
own argument that he had arrived in the east, on the
threshold of 'the Indies'. Both speculations marched
straight off the page of medieval maps. If, instead of
reading Columbus with a modern Mercator projection
map in mind, one reads him with the Psalter map in
view, he cannot any longer be thought mad or deluded.
He emerges as a conventional European man of his
times. The light that led Columbus to the Americas was
not the faint glimmer of imminent modern geography

but the luminous images of medieval maps.

Neither the Dark Ages nor the Middle Ages of Europe were as inward looking and immobile as received history would have us believe. The movement was inexorably toward Jerusalem, the centre of all those medieval maps, and it was summed up in the institutions of pilgrimage and crusade. The son of Henry III, who would have observed the great map at Whitehall, went on crusade in 1271. The pilgrimage to Jerusalem was a continuous European institution. It existed and grew in popularity throughout the Dark Ages and was at its height just before the preaching of the First Crusade by Pope Urban II at Clermont in 1095. His exhortation occasioned a mass response from all strata of European society.

The centuries of the Crusades opened Europe to trade and scholarship, inspired by its contacts with the remnants of the Byzantine Empire and the Muslim world. The Crusades planted a Western European population in a Middle East that was constantly changing, constantly being replenished by a steady stream of travellers. The crusader kingdoms existed for two centuries along with institutions such as the Orders of Knights and the pilgrimage tradition. The ideological correctness of medieval maps was that they inscribed what was happening on the ground, the real interests of travelling people. In their fusion of classical and Christian information and concepts, the maps illustrated the information of concern to the European traveller.

As Chaucer's pilgrims tell us, travellers on the move liked to be entertained by tales. Chaucer's tales also reflect the *oculus mundi* of the medieval world. Indeed,

the great literary classics of the Middle Ages all have a
questing motif centred around or interwoven with the
living institutions of pilgrimage and crusading. The Crusades popularised genres of literature that were by no
means the exclusive property of the literate. The information available to the learned about the earth and its
peoples also made its way into the popular literature.

Literary conventions were another means by which
the ideological contents of medieval maps spread throughout Europe. The chansons de geste, the performance
literature of the medieval balladeers, such as the *Chanson
de Roland*, gave the contemporary Crusades a history,
locating their motifs, concerns and rationale by harking
back to the time of Charlemagne when the Muslim tide
had been turned back from the heartlands of Europe. The
chansons de geste mingled with the Arthurian romances,
the other popular medieval tradition of literature. Celtic
in origin, the Arthurian romances became the common
stock of European literature. They were the epitome of
the medieval chivalric ideal, an encyclopedic vehicle that
served as the manual of manners and mores for the
courtly society of the late Middle Ages, and as a guide to
its ideology and knowledge base. Likewise, the legend of
Prince Henry the Navigator as the exemplary scientific
inquirer (probably instigated by Henry himself) derived
from the *Chronicle* of Gomes Eanes de Azurara. The
latter employed all the motifs of the chivalric literary
genre laden with its questing, crusading overtones.

The central theme of the Arthurian romances, concerned as it was with the quest for Christian perfection,
was deeply infused with notions of pilgrimage and
crusade. Its characters were always on the move through

the geographic extent of the world. This whole tradition was replete with conventional, medieval notions about history, geography and anthropology.

Some of the Arthurian tales included Celtic and Norse geographic knowledge under the guise of Arthur's reputed conquests of the known world. The general European diffusion of this genre was a fitting memorial to the importance of the Celtic fringes, where Celtic Christianity kept scholarship alive during the Dark Ages.

One of the most careful scholars of that era, one who preserved and maintained geographic knowledge, was the Venerable Bede. Though he rarely moved out from the confines of his monastery in Northumbria, this impaired his learning not at all. The darkness of the Dark Ages is largely characterised by the general decline in knowledge of Greek, yet the main classical sources current in the Middle Ages also constituted the bulk of the scholarship of the Dark Ages.

Both of these eras emphasised preservation of information. Neither had anything comparable to the modern sense of history and time, in that their sense of history and time carried no connotation of change. They saw historical events as a map of ideological concerns, a demonstration of matters of enduring and timeless importance. Central to the symbolism of history and literary convention was the moral drama of human existence, the supreme importance of the chivalric quest for eternal salvation through proper and correct identification of and response to the demonic and the divine. All knowledge and information was significant in so far as it fed into or derived from that Christian moral context.

This Celtic 'fringe' spawned two persistent traditions that spoke of Celtic 'discoveries' of America centuries before Columbus. The Irish St Brendan, active in the seventh century but whose legend dates from the ninth century, possibly got to Iceland before the Vikings. Irishmen certainly did so. The saint's quest for Hy Brazil, the Island of the Blessed, somewhere in the Atlantic, figures on most medieval maps. It should not be confused with modern-day Brazil since the name of the Saint's island is a corruption of *breas ail*, which can be translated as either 'fortunate' of 'blessed' isle. (Both terms are found on maps. The Brazilian nation got its name, prosaically, from brazil wood, a source of red dye.)

The voyages of St Brendan are in the questing genre and were possibly imaginary. The real message of St Brendan however, is the significance of the interior quest for Christian understanding. Though this message was conveyed through the context of actual Irish seafaring, its topical and real historical references did not prejudice its attraction or success as devotional literature.

Madoc, Prince of Gwynedd, the Welsh claimant to the 'discovery' of America, is a more spurious but instructive legend. It is probable, though the evidence is sparse, that Madoc did exist in popular tradition in medieval Wales. But the beginnings of the legend were probably inspired by Mercator himself through judicious use of his own *oculus mundi*. The Madoc myth first appears in print in Britain around 1579 after a comment made by the Dutch geographer on the subject in a letter to the exotic Welsh scholar Dr John Dee. So impressed was Dr Dee that he proceeded immediately to urge Elizabeth I to lay claim to the whole of North America on the basis of Madoc having landed there in 1170. The Welsh-speaking queen was, after all, the current representative of a Welsh dynasty, the Tudors. Her grandfather, Henry VII, whom Columbus had sought to interest in his schemes for discovery, had consciously sought to legitimise his tenuous claim to the throne of England by employing his Celtic–British credentials, not least through naming his first born son Arthur, the same Arthur he sought to marry to the daughter of Ferdinand and Isabella, Catherine of Aragon.

In European thought, as the historian Gwyn A. Williams (1979) has so persuasively argued, the real historical quest is not for the truth or falsity contained in a specific legend. The measure of the importance of medieval history, geography, myth or fabulous travellers' tales lies not in their empirical accuracy or error but in their capacity to be acted upon as if they were real, in their capacity to set empirical events underway. The significance of myth and literature, or even of cartography and cosmology, is that they cannot be read solely as a store of empirical knowledge. They are also categories of thought and understanding through which empirical encounters are expressed.

None of the errors contained in medieval sources, of which later commentators make so much, are significant simply as errors, and this is why admitting that they were errors often took an awfully long time, even in the face of compelling empirical experience. Well into the early nineteenth century travellers were still searching for Welsh-speaking Indians, scions of Madoc's planting in the Americas. We find no less a rationalist than Thomas Jefferson, whose family originated in Madoc country in North Wales, instructing the explorers Lewis and Clark to look for these mythical Welsh Indians.

So minuscule indeed was Columbus's hold on what is known of the globe today that it prevented him even from identifying his transatlantic landing as a continent unknown to Europe. Columbus was sufficiently appraised of the cutting edge of Renaissance thinking to suspect that he had encountered a new continent, but so powerful was the hold of *oculus mundi* that it was more pragmatic and plausible for him to insist that he had arrived on the edge of Asia, that his islands were the gateway to the Indies by a shorter, direct route.

Thus, the personal or psychological profile of Christopher Columbus is less important that the cultural and ideological personality of European Christendom through which he operated. Individual life histories can divert attention from the generality and commonplaces of history. They render possible an easier (or kinder) construction of the past by providing easy scapegoats. If the past can be reduced to the failings of an individual, the complicity of an entire culture and its participation in that individual's misdeeds need never come under scrutiny. What happened in America, and in the Americas, the reflected impact of America on European ideas, and the manner in which America came to inform Europe's relations with the whole world, can never be summed up in the life history of one individual, whether hero or villain.

The motivations and history, the *oculus mundi* of the whole of Europe, stood behind Columbus's get-rich-quick scheme. If anything revolutionary emerged from his undertaking later, as in the case of his contemporary Copernicus, it did so because of the essentially medieval cast of his ideas and information. The work of the Polish priest overturned Europe's geo-centric view of the universe, yet he has been described as the last great Ptolemaic astronomer. Columbus, whose exploits re-shaped the European conception of the terrestrial globe, could have such an impact because he too was a student of Ptolemy, who had shaped so much of the medieval European image of the world.

Copernicus and Columbus are heralded as luminaries of the Renaissance. This is one of their main claims to fame. However, when applauding the Renaissance as the first triumph of modernity and as the end of the medieval, it may be useful to remember the historian, J.R. Hale's (1971) cautionary note, that the impact of the early Renaissance on European thought was to increase its deference to precisely those classical sources that were the common currency of medieval scholarship and European information.

The Renaissance was a shift of style and emphasis, a change in fashion. The intellectual building blocks of modernity during the Renaissance tied Europeans more firmly to their medieval roots. These blocks represented a continuity that could be passed off as profound change. Thus it was the medieval spirit of inquiry, and its scholastic techniques applied to classical sources, that began the enterprise of the Indies. It was a case of old ideas making new departures when Columbus set sail from the port of Palos on 3 August 1492.

For Columbus, his inherited myths were the real charter that set historic events in motion, and not merely in terms of the geographic idea that there was a place out there to get to, but also in terms of the people one was likely to encounter once one arrived. Accompanying

him was not merely a whole iconography, but also a
mental geography that included an anthropology of barbarism. The latter had its origins not in the medieval ages in
Europe but rather in the earlier civilisations of Greece
and Rome, and the Judeo–Christian tradition to which
Europe became heir.

2 THEM

THE FOUNDATIONS ON WHICH Western civilisation –
its attitudes to nature and to people living beyond its
frontiers – is grounded, were primarily set not by classical
Greece but by the biblical tradition, from the interpretation of the struggle for survival of the Israelites recorded in
the Old Testament. Even a casual reading of the Old
Testament suggests an unambiguous view of the earth as
hostile and of the duty of humanity to subdue it to their
ends by force. Adam's punishment in the Genesis myth is
to remain in exile from the Garden of Eden. Man enters
the wilderness of the world, estranged forever from nature.
Nature, in fact, becomes a cursed adversary, eternally
hostile to man's efforts at survival. Adam is also fated to be
an enemy of the animals. Human existence in this world
takes on the character of an unremitting contest with
nature in which man toils to fulfil God's command that he
subdue the thorny, thistled earth and establish dominion
over it.

Subsequent Old Testament events have the cumulative
effect of re-emphasising this destructive aspect of nature
and of reinforcing the anthropomorphic, adversarial attitude towards the natural world announced in the paradisial
myth. Nature was not a power with which one could
establish a celebratory, reverential relationship. On the
contrary, it was a power from which one sought deliver-
ance. Nature had to be subdued, controlled and put to
better use by man's efforts.

The God of the Israelites was perceived as completely

detached from nature: though he had created it, he was not to be found everywhere in it. If nature existed, it was merely as an instrument for the creator as a means to display his power. Compare this attitude with Islam's in which nature remains sacred as can be determined by a reading of any Sufi scholar such as Jalaluddin Rumi, Sadi Shirazi, ibn Arabi or Farid al Din Attar. A similarly hostile attitude was mandated against other gods and the sacred notions of other cultures: they were to be seen as adversaries to the true god, and destroyed. Intolerance and commands to destroy the sacred items of Others is incorporated in Judaic monotheism and was passed on to Christianity. Biblical history was appropriated by Christianity, for which it became the actual explanation, in literal and conceptual terms, of the origins and purpose of the universe and man's place in it. In this sense the Mosaic heritage became integral to the West and formed part of the equipment Westerners took with them as they thrust out into the undiscovered beyond.

The second pillar of Western civilisation, derived from classical Greece, contained similar distinctions, particularly concerning separateness from Other People, and served to reinforce the first pillar. It is from the Greeks that Europe acquired the concept of the barbarian. The word, which comes from *barbaroi*, can be translated as 'babbler' or someone who could not speak Greek. For the Greeks such an inability in any person or race betrayed predominantly a negative human condition because language was the tool of reason. To say that some people could not speak Greek was to imply they had no faculty of reason and could not act according to logic; that their intellect was poorly developed and unable to control their passions; and that while they could apprehend reason they could not have possession of true reason. The term *barbaroi* was therefore applied to all non-Greek speaking people.

The Greeks were a trading and travelling people and their scholars great systematisers. So in their geography and history are collated many tales of distant peoples. In fact, a large part of the medieval iconography of Otherness is a direct transmission of ideas, accompanied by geographical eclecticism, that originated with the Greeks.

The primal character in the Greek history of Otherness is Cyclops, the giant Polyphemos who captures Odysseus and his men in the founding Greek text, the Odyssey of Homer. Polyphemos inhabits caves. He is a gargantuan individual, has only one eye, and is also a cannibal. He possesses articulate speech, yet suffers a lack of 'civic institutions', religion and technological advancements such as agriculture and shipbuilding. He is also the origin of the legend of the wild man, a persistent figure of ancient and medieval thought. More importantly, the list of attributes by which Polyphemos is described and located reads like the pattern book not only of medieval thought but also of the analytic categories that swayed the minds of Columbus and his successors.

Polyphemos occurs in myth, which is the magico-religious charter of Greek civilisation. Within the mythic structure of understanding he inhabits the Golden Age, the age prior to the ordering of the contemporary world of the Greeks. The Golden Age is doubly golden in character: it is an age both of innocence and wealth. So, linked with the notion of monstrous races are the aura and the lure of gold and riches that are easily acquired, at the extreme edges of the travelled lands.

The Greeks thus very early established the outer dimensions of what later became the European debate about human nature and anthropology. The categories and attributes of humanity they employed to think about themselves and about non-Greeks have endured in Western thought. It was the Greeks who introduced the pygmies; the *Kynokephaloi*, the dog-headed people; the *Skiapodes*, the shadow-footed people; the *Akepheloi*, the people with no head and with their eyes on their chest; as well as the *Cyclops*, the people with only one eye. Greek literature is also replete with hybrid races: minotaurs, centaurs and satyrs. The monstrosity of Other Peoples the physical character of their being, is a direct corollary of the difference of their lifestyle and behaviour from the Greek norm. Together, they define the barbarism without.

The notion of barbarous people who live a communal life is also old; to the hierarchic Greeks, even when they were democrats, this communal life indeed was the ultimate in Otherness. It goes back to Homer and the Abioi, a people who have a vegetarian diet and are noted not only for their justness but also for the communism they practise. It was just as remarkable a concept when it burst upon Europe in the wake of Columbus as a feature of the New World.

Greek writers had thus collected a whole series of distinguishing characteristics that marked off the barbarians. These characteristics centred around dietary practises, sexual customs and cultural faculties, and had a symmetrical play of opposition that Hartog (*Le Miroir d'Herodote*) argued should be seen as differences that are 'good to think with' or useful as a culture's 'navigational aids'. Much modern scholarship, on the other hand, has attempted to unravel the identities of these 'barbarians', viewing their existence in literature as garbled descriptions of actual lost tribes.

The first report of this genre describing the people of India, for instance, was produced by Scylax of Caryanda, a Greek officer sent by Darius of Persia around 515BC to explore the newly conquered eastern portion of his empire, (the Indus valley). Scylax reported that the huge quantities of gold available to the Indians came from giant anthills to be found in the northern deserts. His descriptions of people were even more fantastic; some of the Indians, he wrote, had such enormous feet they would lie on the ground and use them as an umbrella over their heads. The Indians in the extreme south, he reported, were cannibals. The great compendium maker of this large and varied tradition of fantastic reporting was Herodotus, whom the West calls the 'father of history'. While the pre-Herodotan tradition had its pygmies in India, Herodotus located them in the interior of Africa. As for the Indian cannibals, these were now transferred to the Persian frontier. The eclecticism is neither arbitrary nor irrational, but a sign of enduringly important demarcations that unite phenomena in the common sphere of Otherness formed by cross-cultural contact. The monstrous races persist through time, despite increasing or decreasing contact, because they persistently represent distinctions that must be borne in mind. Ctesias of Cnidus, a critic of Herodotus, went a step further. The author of two separate treatises, one on Persia, the other on India, Ctesias portrayed the Indians as satyrs. His account was passed on to the Middle Ages via Pliny.

When Alexander of Macedon launched his bid for world

domination he travelled east, accompanied by an entire
coterie of experts who were to investigate and record these
far-off lands. (Centuries later, when Napoleon Bonaparte
began his invasion of Egypt he took just such a party of
scientific camp followers with him, from which we date the
modern rise of Orientalism.) Few of the works of Cal-
listhenes, Ptolemy and Aristoboulos, the experts who
accompanied Alexander, survive but they spawned an
antique Orientalism in the powerful Alexandrian romance
genre. This genre firmly locates the monstrous races in
India and the Indies. A second source for the Indian
connection is Megasthenes, sent by Seleucis as an emissary
to the court of Chandragupta in the fourth century BC. He
included in his reports the familiar litany of monstrous
races, and added a few new ones.

What has been recounted above concerning the Greeks
could be repeated for the Romans. Rome of the Republic
and of the Empire was also a hierarchic society, jealous of
its citizenship to such an extent that not even the extension
of citizenship could blur the importance of the *boni*, the
good people, as essentially the corpus of ancient patrician
families. The Roman world was more extensive than either
its Greek predecessor or its medieval successor.

Pomponius Mela, the earliest Latin geographer of the
period whose work is available, revived the wild stories of
Amazons, griffons and headless peoples. He also invented
the legends of Chryse and Argyre beyond India: the soil of
the former was of gold, the latter of silver. These formed
the first notions of prosperous lands to the east and, later,
the conception of the Golden Chersonese (The Malay
peninsula) which would figure in the discourse of the
Middle Ages.

The other influential geographer was Ptolemy of Alexandria, whose maps, as we have already seen, gained a new lease of life in the Middle Ages and eventually directed the explorations of Columbus.

Rome pushed the troglodytes further and further into the interior of Africa with the expansion of trans-Saharan trade until they reached the goldfields of sub-Saharan West Africa. And Rome had no end of problems with savages. It is from the Roman horror and fear of the people of the woods, the barbarian tribes of northern and eastern Europe that we derive the very notion of savages, from *sylvan*, the *sauvage*, the peoples of the forest. The city of Rome existed for centuries with the lurking fear that savages would sweep out of the forests to murder its citizens in their beds. Finally, having variously fought and civilised its savages, Rome eventually fell to savage outsiders.

The highly unflattering portrayals left behind by Rome coloured historical perceptions of the invaders for centuries. The Goths, Visi or Ostra, and the Vandals and other barbarians who inherited the rubble of the empire, were desperate to accommodate Roman culture, not to destroy it. Nevertheless, they received a bad press from unregenerate, patrician, late Roman writers. Roman literature is full of horrendous accounts of the savagery of savages. Tacitus gives us the classic account of the wood religion of the Druids, the Celtic religion of the oak grove, with the most lurid, blood-curdling references to their use of Stonehenge for human sacrifice. Contemporary archaeology reveals this to be a superb piece of propaganda. Tacticus's account is no more lurid than Spanish accounts of Aztec ceremonies, and no doubt served the same functions. To establish the ideology of Otherness in order to buttress its notion of civilisation, Rome had not only apocryphal tales of its own encounters with savages but also the legacy of the monstrous races acquired from the Greeks. Greek scholarship was the foundation of the education and the cultivated life of Rome. This whole corpus combined in the work of Pliny the Elder, who died in AD79, but whose *Historia Naturalias* was a standard work throughout the Middle Ages. (A heavily annotated copy was in the library of Christopher Columbus.) Pliny covered the whole of the known world in 13 books, each with a similar structure, three of which cover Scythia, Africa and the Orient. For Pliny, Ethiopia was a new location for unregenerate monstrosity, and many of the familiar monstrous races make their appearance there. In the seventh book he collected all the fabulous and monstrous tales he could find, and it is this seventh book, published separately in the Middle Ages, that had an enormous impact on the Western imagination. Here, Ethiopia and India vie for distinction as the locale of monstrous races who appear in a profusion of names and attributes.

There is a direct parallel between the accounts of Pliny and Herodotus. In both, the monstrous races belong to a system of concentric circles that have their centres in Italy or Greece. As one moves away from the centre the inhabitants become wilder, and regional specificity becomes less important. At the extremes of wilderness – in Ethiopia, Scythia and India – the two texts become one. So the historic concentric circle that moves from Athens to Rome, from fifth century BC to first century AD , contains the same ideological conception of human nature and the diversity to which it can give rise. The reference is always the human nature at the centre, the defining civilisation against which the degree of wildness, barbarity and savagery is determined through the comparative narration of essential attributes. Behind all the interwoven threads stands the necessity to fashion an ideological dividing line between the civilised and the uncivilised.

As familiar to Ptolemy as they were to the last Ptolemaic seafarer, the monstrous Plinian peoples were a consistent part of the medieval European heritage. With the increased authority of the classical sources as part of the context of the Renaissance, Columbus's reliance on the convention of the Plinian peoples was no medieval obscurantism, as so many writers today are fond of believing.

The original message of Christianity concerned the divinity that dwells within and that is present in all creation, and how to live in accordance with this. Yet in the historical interpretation of Jesus in the vast industry of Christology, the emphasis shifted from the message to the historical figure, who was now presented as having once intervened in the history of this world only to show it as the contemptible thing it truly was; who had assumed flesh only to show that it was possible to live beyond the body, to subordinate its desires to the utterly different needs of the spirit. This transformation is most obvious in the celebrated conversion of St Paul, where conversion is equated with a kind of on-going self-slaughter. No wonder St Paul has often been referred to as the inventor of Christianity. Here begins in New Testament scripture the fatal divorce between body and soul, between nature and religion, that has come to seem the very essence of the Christian faith. This development has had incalculable consequences for the history of the West, and through exploration and settlement, for the rest of the globe.

These anti-nature tendencies continued to grow through the desert fathers. Legend has it that one saint became so ashamed of having a body at all that each time he ate or satisfied any other bodily need he would blush. Another desert father, Rufinus of Aquileia, could describe his encounter with cave drawings of ancient animal deities as an engagement with the very essence of that evil he had been sent to the desert to combat.

Turned away from nature, Christian history now becomes a steadily lengthening chronicle of mass neurosis. The hatred for the body deepens and is most notable in the gory punishments inflicted by the mystics. All this aggression against the body, against the natural world, against primitives, heretics, all unbelievers, is exercised in the vain, tragic, pathetically maintained hope of thereby strengthening weak belief and winning paradise.

In the Middle Ages, the wild man (and his mate, the wild woman), with his classical and barbarian antecedents also returns. The thread of Cyclops, related to the gods, inhabitant of the innocence of the Golden Age, gets enmeshed with the vague European memories of the older patterns of learning of the Celtic and Germanic peoples. These memories, images, perceptions are overlaid with Old Testament and Christian perceptions and with the demonic associations of underworld shaggy creatures, with earth, sex, blood and sin. As Satan mocked the civilised Christian world and its institutions and sought to confuse by aping it, so the wild women (learned in the lore of both medicine and magic) become the model for witches.

It is hard not to see this potent image of the naked,

hairy, club-wielding brute as a projection of all that
European civility tried to distance from itself. (Shakespeare's Caliban in *The Tempest* is a good example.)
Tainted by its ancestry, redeemed by its providential
possession of Christianity, there was every reason for
Europe to be highly conscious of the need to demarcate
the boundaries between civil and uncivil, between the good
people and the barbarian, between Us and Them.

The medieval fascination with the wild man was that he
could potentially exist within the bounds of Europe itself,
within the individual himself as a lurking force, always
threatening to overcome and destroy him. The wild man
had therefore to be either civilised or sacrificed to
civilisation. He could hardly be allowed to remain his
brutish and unrepentant self, since as such he directly
opposed the imperative extension of order. As we have
seen from the Hereford and Psalter maps, the Bible is
once again the principal source of geographical knowledge.
Paradise is located in Asia, at the eastern frontier of the
world. The major rivers, the Indus, the Nile and Euphrates,
are thought to have a common source in the Garden of
Eden. In the literature circulating during the ninth to the
eleventh centuries the familiar background of dog-headed
people and weird animals is resumed. India is now
populated by horned pygmies who become old in seven
years, while the Brahmans commit suicide by fire or eat
their old parents to do them honour. The accounts of
Ctesias or Alexander's experts are Christianised, embel-
lished with biblical allegories and fresh fantasies, and also
gradually penetrate the popular literature of the crusading
era.

By the end of the eleventh century the tradition of the

church militant founded by St Augustine had turned
outward. St Augustine established the central importance
of orthodox belief as the civil basis of Roman Christian
society. Drawing on the verse in the Gospel of Luke (4:23)
'Compel them to come in', his horror of heresy became
what Paul Johnson (1978) has termed a doctrine of
'constructive persecution'. The doctrine became the cutting
edge of a clear ideological line between We and They
around which all the marks of Otherness that Western
civilisation had inherited were arrayed and deployed.

The Crusades truly start the pattern of large-scale,
international Christian violence against all unbelievers that
bears fruit in the ruins of the Aztec capital Tenochtitlan.
The ceremonial centre of the Mexican capital was reduced
to burning rubble before Christian churches were raised to
witness the dismemberment and domination of another
civilisation. The First Crusade was preached by Pope
Urban at Clermont at the end of November 1095. Its first
major slaughter, however, was not against the Muslims but
against the Jewish communities at Worms, Mainz and Trier.
The first confrontation in the Middle East was at Antioch,
primarily a Christian city. Muslim chroniclers of the period
recoiled in horror at the ferocity of the crusaders and in
amazement that they would turn their violence on their
co-religionists.

When crusaders reached Jerusalem, William, Archbishop of Tyre (*Historia Rerum in Partibus Transmarinis
Gestarum*, twelfth century), wrote:

> They laid low, without distinction, every enemy encoun-
> tered. Everywhere was frightful carnage, everywhere lay
> heaps of severed heads, so that soon it was impossible to
> pass or to go from one place to another except over the
> bodies of the slain. Already the leaders had forced their

way by various routes almost to the center of the city and wrought unspeakable slaughter as they advanced. A host of people followed in their train, a thirst for the blood of the enemy and wholly intent upon destruction.

Even the victors experienced sensations of horror and loathing:

It was impossible to look upon the vast numbers of the slain without horror; everywhere lay fragments of human bodies, and the very ground was covered with the blood of the slain. It was not alone the spectacle of headless bodies and mutilated limbs strewn in all directions that roused the horror of all who looked on them. Still more dreadful was it to gaze upon the victors themselves, dripping with blood from head to foot, an ominous sight which brought terror to all who met them. It is reported that within the Temple enclosure alone about ten thousand infidels perished, in addition to those who lay slain everywhere throughout the city in the streets and squares, the number of whom was estimated as no less.

But it went on:

The rest of the soldiers roved through the city in search of wretched survivors who might be hiding in the narrow portals and byways to escape death. These were dragged out into public view and slain like sheep. Some formed into bands and broke into houses where they laid violent hands on the heads of families, their wives, children, and their entire households. These victims were either put to the sword or dashed headlong on the ground from some elevated place so that they perished miserably. Each marauder claimed as his own in perpetuity the particular house which he had entered, together with all it contained. For before the capture of the city the pilgrims had agreed that, after it had been taken by force, whatever each man might win himself

should be his forever by right of possession, with
molestation. Consequently the pilgrims searched the city
most carefully and boldly killed the citizens.

The Crusades continued, though it was clear they were not
achieving the purpose of spiritual renewal. In the Middle
East they withered even as a project of military domination.
Jerusalem was lost in 1187, never to be regained despite
three more officially proclaimed Crusades. The imperative
to achieve earthly mastery, to enforce orthodox belief and
to contend with other faiths that offended Christianity by
what Thomas Aquinas dubbed their 'invincible ignorance',
remained. The tangible results of crusading were far less
significant than the catalyst they provided for Western
civilisation. The crusading ethos canalised and brought
together many diverse strands of Western thought and
experience and shaped the content and psychic geography
of the West, complete with its vision of Other People. It
was under the impact of the Crusades that Western Europe
began to acquire its modern form. Perhaps the most telling
legacy of the crusading era was the inextricable connections
it build in the Western mind between religious orthodoxy
and a uniform pattern of living. To deviate from orthodoxy
was heresy; to be different was anathema. Whether in
Europe or beyond, the only reliable citizen was the person
who lived according to the dictates of the Church of Rome.
Beyond that defined ambit lay the wilderness.

The two pillars of Western civilisation, classicism and
Christianity, shared a triumphalist self image. Each
invented Otherness to define itself and the process of
maintaining boundaries required the perennial reinvention
of real peoples.

What it was to be Greek, to be Roman or to be Christian

was a matter of convention. It was made evident when
tracing similarities and differences with the manners and
mores of non-citizens, people who lived outside the Roman
Empire, or people who were not Christians. Real people
became object lessons for 'normality' by their shocking
ability to live differently. Dwelling on the differences and
similarities, extracting pen-portraits of the characteristics
of the Others, was a process of distortion, one that became
more garbled as distance increased, or as contact with
Other cultures became more tenuous or non-existent. But
the most distorting feature of the process of recognition of
Otherness was a function neither of distance nor of
contact. It was derived from the most salient points, the
most central ideas, or what it was to be Greek, Roman or
Christian. It was self-identity that generated the essential
points of comparison. The points of comparison generate
real boundaries, points at which variety becomes something Other, not Us. The very techniques of comparison, as
they have been used by Western scholars since Columbus,
are a process of translation, with all the potential of
distortion that this includes. The beliefs and manners of
Other People become comprehensible when read off
against the practices of the describing civilisation, the very
civilisation that does not share them. Thus the first
Portuguese visitors to India describe a Hindu temple as if
it were a Catholic church. The conventions of a Catholic
church are no safe guide to interpreting Hindu convention;
it only made the wide areas of misrepresentation the
substance of Western understanding, the very stuff of their
discourse about what it was to be a Hindu. The good
citizen would never do such things as Other People did;
the bad citizen might do things even the Indian or

Ethiopian or Moor or Jew or native of Brazil would not
think of doing. The process throws the conventional
normality of 'our' civilisation into sharp relief, while it casts
a negative shade over 'their' ways.

As people well infected with the ideas of their time,
Christopher Columbus and his contemporaries were not
new to this process of construction. However, the process
of generating Otherness now made a new departure and
from the fateful watershed of Columbus's first landfall in
the Americas, became a global project. The further out
from the European mainland, the more distorted and
fictional the shapes of the world became; Western tendency
was to consider *terra incognita* as being either empty or
demonic.

By the century of Columbus, Western civilisation was
possessed of deep-set long-established attitudes towards
the wilderness and indeed towards all unimproved nature,
towards those who lived in the wilderness, and towards the
relationship of 'civilisation' to these. Attitudes now crystal-
ised, paving the way for the transformation of society itself.

It is useful here to shed some light on the Spain of
Christopher Columbus. Muslim Spain had been the only
multicultural society in which Jews, Muslims and Christians
lived in relative harmony. The final defeat and expulsion of
the Moors, after a protracted and savage racial-religious
war of eight centuries and 3,000 battlefields, changed all
that. This left enduring scars on the Spanish psyche. The
victorious completion of the *reconquista* left the social order
with a vacuum of employment and purpose. The first
response to victory over Granada was an initial move to rid
Spanish society of its multiplicity, by the expulsion of the
Jews. They were given a simple ultimatum either to convert

or to go. The date on which this edict came into force was 2 August 1492 – the day before Columbus set sail from the port of Palos. Within a year of the fall of Granada, Spain had acquired a new *conquista*, the vacuum was seamlessly filled, and conquistadores were preparing to set off for *otro mundo*, another world. Even the hand that signed the sailing orders of the Admiral of the Ocean Sea was the same hand that signed the ultimatum to the Jews, that of Juan de Coloma. Now, in 1492, Columbus possessing the essential mind of the West with all its twisted religiosity, its background of classical geography and medieval folklore, and its recent acquisitions of technical skills, was ready to seek out new worlds. During his lifetime the Indies would thus inevitably become the New World analogue of the Crusades. Here, once again, under the cover of righteous Christian outreach, criminal rapaciousness would be sanctioned.

3 DEADLY ENCOUNTER

THE MOMENT COLUMBUS secured land across the Atlantic he began to exercise the power of domination he had been granted by royal warrant and papal pronouncement. He was now a viceroy of somewhere and he located his territory by naming it within European convention; his first landfall he called San Salvador, in honour of Christ the Saviour. The entire modern map of the Americas stands witness to the arrival of the European Christian vision to re-order and relocate its geography. Columbus went on to name subsequent landfalls after the Spanish monarchs Ferdinand and Isabella, and after Spain, their nation.

Yet it is the Christian terminology that figures most prominently in the new destinations created by Columbus. Most frequent are his references to the Holy Trinity – Trinidad – to which he had dedicated his voyages, in conventional medieval fashion, and for which he had a special reverence. The only general term he ever used for the Indies was *otro mundo* – another world. The sea whose geography he unquestionably made known in a modern sense, he named the Caribbean, after the Caribs, a people he determined were cannibal.

Columbus arrived, as he had anticipated, in a populated land. He hoped the peoples he met would lead him to the gold he sought, or to the court of the Great Khan. He also expected that they would unfold for him the world of the Indies as represented in medieval European literature.

Though his enduring claim to the status of discoverer is

in the very Otherness of the peoples he made known to
Europe, his discovery eventually reduced itself to a
conscious work of creative invention through which Indians
were fabricated anew out of a historic set of medieval
European ideas. Faced with real people whose manners
and mores were beyond his experience, he set about
charting their similarities and differences, employing the
anthropology of medieval Christendom and its convention
of the monstrous races, and using Europe as the base and
norm for comparison. From the storehouse of the ideolo-
gies, imageries and expectations of medieval conventions
employed in describing Arawak and Taino, Columbus
invented people other than the Arawak and Taino he
encountered.

It is usual to stress Columbus's sympathetic first
accounts of the inhabitants of the Caribbean islands. When
read against the iconography of barbarism he brought with
him, however, a different picture emerges. In such a picture
there is no enigma in how Columbus, in his role as Viceroy
of the Ocean Sea and all it contained, could depict the
people as innocent inhabitants of a terrestrial paradise and
simultaneously speculate on the riches to be gained by
enslaving them. Thus, lavish in his accounts of the
tractability of the people he invented as Indians, when the
demands of the Spaniards caused friction he was equally
swift to adduce evidence of their barbarous condition.
When these mythical Indians defied or opposed the
invaders they were the fierce, wild Caribs, cannibals to a
man, woman and child.

Cannibalism was one of the standard traits of barbarians
in all Greek, Roman and medieval accounts. It was a
condition to be expected along with a lack of civic

attributes. The occurrence of opposition would inevitably lead to the Taino being questioned about the nature and practices of those Others who declined to serve the Spaniards. In the absence of a common language, and the Hebrew and Aramaic of Columbus's official interpreter being inadequate, it was inevitable that the incomprehensible answers of the Taino should be translated as detailed accounts of institutionalised cannibalism. The most elaborate account was provided by Diego Alvares Chanca, the ship's doctor who accompanied Columbus on his second voyage. Chanca's tale of people herded ready for the pot, of women kept like battery hens to produce youngsters for the pot, of boys emasculated for fattening to make them plump and tender like capons, was widely recycled and a natural for illustration. Its imagery remained alive and potent in European discourse for centuries.

Such graphic images of cannibalism are an inescapable part of all the early sources on the Americas. One early illustration shows a stall constructed of palm fronds where a man, depicted like some burgher butcher, is chopping up bodies and hanging up cuts of human flesh – heads, arms and thighs – for display. This image recurs three centuries later, reproduced in William Arens's book, *The Man Eating Myth* (1979), as representing the European view of African cannibalism in the nineteenth century. Despite persistence, as Arens makes clear, there has never been any reliable evidence for the existence of culturally constituted cannibalism. Europeans asked the questions and recorded the 'responses' in their journals and diaries, and the myth was maintained. The issue, however, is not that the case for cannibalism has not been proven, as even the West's own fair, open-minded and objective writers today tend to assert, it is that the question of cannibalism is actually a question about the European mind and its power to 'overwrite' the world. This issue has never been addressed, let alone answered.

These early images of cannibalism had a gross impact on the European imagination because they were coded messages of great sophistication that employed familiar symbols to represent and refer to ideas that pre-dated contact with the Americas, ideas that were already a familiar part of European discourse. The pictures say far more about the European worldview and its extant notions of the boundary between itself, the true civil society, and all others, than any previous texts describing the peoples of the East Indies. The Indies was not a particular locale. It was in many senses the general term for everything that was not Europe. It lay to the south and east of Europe, as illuminated on all those medieval maps.

The same woodcuts kept being re-used: many of the illustrations used for early accounts of the Americas were swiftly amended versions of woodcuts that had previously been used for texts that had nothing to do with the Americas. There was nothing strange or aberrant about this. The account of the Americas sent off by Chanca to the City Council of Seville were based, as Chanca himself related, on the testimony of a former captive woman picked up at sea, who was interviewed when the interpreter (such as he was) was absent.

In his study of how the classical and medieval legacy was utilised to represent the New World, Peter Mason (1990) picks out, as one example, Diodoros's account of Iamboulos, a traveller who voyaged to the seven islands of the Heliopolitans, a people supposedly located in the regions of India. The Heliopolitans are responsible for the legend of El Dorado and the seven cities of gold, for which both Sir Walter Raleigh and Coronado searched in vain in the Americas. (The explorers never found the cities but they did bring huge tracts of territory into European orbit.) The Heliopolitans, according to Iamboulos, have hairless bodies, are very tall, live to the age of 150 years, have their women in common and are extremely versatile in the reproduction off all kinds of sound, including bird song.

As Mason notes, many of these features reappear in *Novus Mundi*, Amerigo Vespucci's account of the Amerindians, a work that was widely circulated around 1504. Vespucci used predictable Greek sources that described of course, totally imaginary people. Vespucci also pirated the claim to 'discovery' of the New World and gave his name to the new continent: America. Not only can we trace the modern tradition of anthropology to fictions in Vespucci's *Novus Mundi*, but the book is also the main source for Thomas More's *Utopia* and the entire modern tradition of utopian social thought. Thus, fiction begot fiction and provided Europe with two ways of looking at the Other: anthropology and utopian thought.

Chanca had elaborated on the institution of cannibalism and made is a salacious item of European discourse. Amerigo Vespucci concentrated on sexual proclivities. Prurience was not a feature of medieval Europe, as the stories told by Chaucer's pilgrims demonstrates, and certainly it was not a feature of the Renaissance. Michaelangelo's vision of the Christian story of creation spread over the ceiling of the Sistine chapel acquired breeches only after the Reformation. Vespucci's observations and reports were part of the common and necessary list of inquiries into the outward manifestation of the inherent human nature of the people he encountered.

Anthropological self-examination in recent years has shown how questions predicate answers. The questions bring the worldview of the questioner, with all its conventional knowledge-base, into play and determine what the questioner hears and notes down as an answer. Contemporary anthropology begins with the accounts of Columbus and the first European visitors to the Americas. However, their questions and observations were shaped by the anthropology of barbarism of the classical world and medieval Christendom: hair flowing down an Amerindian back, the use of the bow and arrow, sexual profligacy and lack of clothing, the existence or absence of religious practices and hierarchical structures, consumption of raw or cooked food. All of these potential similarities with Europeans were used to build up a portrait of difference.

So the category American Indians was constructed out of the European conventions of which these people were negative examples. Again and again in early accounts one reads 'They have no...' What they lacked were the characteristics of the society of Europe. What they possessed was never the concern of their European observers. The effort of the observers was merely to locate them so they could be disposed of following the legal conventions of European life.

To report that people were naked, that they lacked body hair except for long tresses down their backs, that they lacked a sense of property, lacked family institutions and religion, and were artlessly willing to ape the doings of the Spaniards was to locate them intellectually and legally outside the bounds of civil society and to suggest that they had no right over the territory they inhabited. It was to attest that they were fit subjects for enslavement.

Likewise, the use of the notion of the Golden Age was intended not to add lustre to the understanding of the innocence with which the Taino shared what they had with the newcomers, worked for them, and exchanged gold ornaments for dross, but to place them outside civil and legal protection. It was used to render irrelevant the formality of the *requerimiento* Columbus read to them, since no treaty ceding dominion to the Spanish crown was necessary from people who were evidently transient users, not owners in the strict legal sense, of their own lands and goods.

It was not only the Portuguese and the Spanish who held these views. The Englishman Humphrey Gilbert's letters patent (11 June 1578), for example, empowered him to search out remote 'heathen and barbarous' lands not occupied by Christian princes. The locations of these lands are properly vague, but the cultural assumptions are plain: such remote lands belong by right of the true faith to such Christian princes as should first discover them, and not to the native inhabitants. This assumption was never stated outright, of course. In its place, a more benign version was offered, namely, that the Christians had as much right to the wilderness lands as did the natives, indeed a greater right if the latter proved unwilling to share with them. The New World, in plain words, was to be taken.

Gilbert had rendered distinguished service in another English colonising venture, Ireland. Ireland was a sort of apprenticeship for many who would later be engaged in

New World activities, the Irish natives serving the English as the Moors and West Africans had once served the Portuguese and Spanish. Irish campaigns were schoolings in savagery and in them the 'wild Irish' forfeited their lives and lands by reason of cultural differences.

In Humphrey Gilbert and in Sir George Peckham's *A True Report of the Late Discoveries*, (1583), exploration and colonisation became Christian callings. The country newly discovered by the coasting Gilbert is inhabited only by savages without knowledge of the true God. The land was given by God to yield things necessary for man's life. The introduction of Christianity therefore must entail the introduction to the savages of all manner of civilised pursuits including agriculture, necessitating English settlement and English working of the soil:

> That God hath left this honour unto us. The journey knowne, the passage quicklie runne, The land full rich, the people easilie wunne. Whose gaines shalbe the knowledge of our faith, And ours such ritches as the country hath.

Peckham outlines two kinds of planting: The first is one in which the Christians ingratiate themselves with the savages by peaceful and gradual means, offering them gaudy trifles, defending them against the raids of supposed cannibal neighbours, teaching them the faith, and reaping the resulting economic benefits. The second type comes into being when the savages, ungrateful for all this, turn against the Christians in an unlawful attempt to dislodge them from their justly won portion of the New World. When this should happen, says Peckham, 'there is no bar but in stout assemblies, the Christians may issue out, and by strong hand pursue their enemies, subdue them, take possessions of their Towns, Cities or Villages (and in avoiding murderous tyranny) to use the law of arms, as in like case among all nations at this day is used.'

What he meant is that there is only one type of planting; the second is envisioned as the consequence of the inevitable failure of the first. Savages being what they are, they must resist civilisation and Christianity. This was also the logic of the Spanish *requerimiento*. Those who worshipped the earth, the earthy, belonged to the vast company of the damned, while those who steadfastly kept their eyes heavenward might at least hope to belong to the city of God. Between these lay a huge and impassable gulf like that separating body and soul, Dives and Lazarus, or Prospero and his filth.

Thus did the Europeans destroy a whole way of life in the name of civilisation. Not surprisingly, a similar fate was reserved for the natural environment. The natural endowments of the New World were thunderous. The land often announced itself with a heavy scent miles out into the ocean, and the coasting whites, with their nostrils full of salt and sour odours of confinement, recorded their delight in the scents of forests and flowers and cedars, the riot of colour and sound, of game and luxuriant vegetation. Yet, all these vast areas and lands would soon be transformed by the invaders into counterparts of their homelands. They cleared much of the landscape with a driven passion, for 'As long as we keep ourselves busy tilling the earth, there is no fear of any of us becoming wild.'

Living in land so transformed by the burdens they brought, we find it almost incredible that the Americas was so recently an unscarred place of overpowering beauty and fecundity. It had been nurtured by civilisations that demonstrated a genius for horticulture. Despite the over-bearing arrogance of the Europeans who presumed to teach 'agriculture' to the savage natives, the original inhabitants of the Americas continued to nurture the continent long after the European conquest, and have bequeathed to us some of the major staples of a modern diet. The potato, maize, tomato, pumpkin, peanut and cassava head the list of crops domesticated by the peoples of the Americas. In this indigenous facility with the environment there existed a science and sympathy with the natural world that has been eradicated. Now people have some trouble imagining either beauty or fecundity.

What underlay the Europeans' clearing of the continent were the ancient fears and divisions that they brought to the New World along with the primitive precursors of the technology that would assist in transforming the continent. Haunted by these fears, driven by their divisions, they slashed and hacked at the wilderness they saw so that within three centuries of Cortes's penetration of the mainland a world millions of years in the making vanished into the voracious, insatiable maw of an alien civilisation.

The other great theme of the discovery narratives concerns itself with waste and frantic spoliation, an uncontrolled urge to control lands and remove all vestiges of nature. Soon the wilderness was a faded and vaguely disquieting memory, perhaps most in evidence by its negative reminders: vanished forests; erosion; opened, parched lands; and small pockets of aboriginal slums. In the Mississippi Valley 25 million acres of forest a year were destroyed, and the wildlife and fauna exterminated or seriously endangered.

And beneath all of this was that sense so powerfully

urged in the Old Testament, of dark chaos rolled back to the edges of lucid creation, where it crouches waiting to engulf the cleared spaces of human endeavour, as the desert sands of the Near East seemed always to be waiting to sweep again over cultivated lands too long neglected. Order was the cleared and cultivated field or the carefully tended garden, nature made better by man, and it was the obligation of the Christian to bring this order to places deemed to be lacking in it. On such land one might then hope for prosperity.

The problem of how to resolve the ambiguity of the 'newly discovered' space, and particularly its peoples, extant but unknown, knowable but taxing to the conventions of European thought, set the intellectual circles of Europe spinning. The big question of the era was what to make of the place Columbus had actually reached. By 1504 Peter Martyr, philosopher at the court of Ferdinand and Isabella, was arguing that South America was the antipodes, the reputed southern continent.

As more information came back, the lands visited by Columbus began to be mapped. Martin Waldseemuller produced a new world map in 1507, and coined the name 'America' for this new space. He was impressed by Amerigo Vespucci's claim to have recognised a New World across the Atlantic. In both the Americas and the Indies, however, it was the conventional habits of medieval scholarship that were deployed to describe and locate these lands and their peoples, and make them knowable, so that control could be exercised over them. It was a conscious process of invention according to the established norms of European thought, a conscious product of the Christian worldview.

In the Americas the questions posed by this process subjected the unity and universality of this framework to critical assessment for the first time. As Anthony Padgen (1993) points out, all the medieval writing about barbarians and Plinian races had been speculative, a mental construct. It was the Americas that made the speculative actual, and turned it into a mental device that had to be deployed in order to make this new space legitimately subject to European domination.

As a New World came to be established in European understanding the first major issue concerned the origin of its people: how was this to be explained? The only available framework for explanation was the biblical account in Genesis, which established a genealogical connection between all peoples. How could inhabitants of a previously unrecorded continent be part of this genealogy? No one was about to throw out the Genesis account. Indeed, European thought was reluctant to take this leap even in the late nineteenth century, as the outcry against Darwin's theory of evolution made clear. In the sixteenth and seventeenth centuries there were no conceivable alternatives to the ideas, terminology and logical structure of the Christian worldview; they were the only things available to think with. So the peoples of America had to be tacked on to a unitary structure, while the structure in turn was subtly altered to take account of new pragmatic concerns.

The Amerindians came to be thought of as representing the primal simplicity that existed before the flood, or degenerate examples of human regression planted in their new continent after the flood and the dispersal of nations following the fall of the Tower of Babel, genealogically related to the inhabitants of furthest Asia.

By the time the French Huegenot Issac de la Preyere (1594-1676) was writing he could speculate that there had been no universal flood, and hence that there were separate origins for different peoples of the world. Thus the polygenist basis for racism was laid. He argued that there were categories of men, including intermediate groups of humanoids such as nymphs, satyrs, pygmies and wild men, which included the Amerindians, who were descended from a different 'Adam' and hence sundered completely from 'true men', which means primarily Europeans. The fascination with the questions raised by the origin of the Amerindians proposed a conscious inquiry into the origins and status of a humankind that began to reformulate the categories of Christian understanding. Vast quantities of new information was becoming available that exactly fitted the fashion for antiquarian interest in Europe.

The Americas were immensely 'good to think with' at precisely the time when Europe was reforming its understanding of Christianity and hence reopening and shifting its categories of thought. The movement known as the Reformation was prompted by and involved solely with European concerns. It was a search for a purified understanding and practice of the Roman Catholic religion that ended by fracturing the unity of Roman Christianity. To justify and sustain the Protestant vision of Christianity as the true and full meaning of the Bible was not merely a work of theology and spiritual amendment, it had to reopen the entire question of the origin of the purposes of creation and humankind.

The construction of a new Protestant worldview was far more central for Europe than the invention of a New

World and new people. But in the elaboration of that
Protestant vision, the New World and its peoples provided
crucial new possibilities for thinking about human history
as a process of secular changes. The earliest, staunchly
Protestant, settlers in North America regarded the rapid
spread of death and disease that decimated the Amerindian
populations as providential – the work of providence in
clearing the path for its chosen elect to follow their calling
in a new land. It was true proof of their calling, of the
superiority of Protestantism over the heresies of Popery,
because it was not the experience of that most Popish of
Empires, the Spanish, further south in the New World.

The essence of Protestantism was to conceive of itself as
representing the providential rise of human society to a
new, more complete, more correct understanding of the
meaning and purpose of creation. Protestantism reformulated the European conception of authority: religious,
intellectual, social and political. The fathers of theology, the
early founders of Christianity, were shown to have been in
error by new philological studies of early Greek gospel
texts. The ancients, the classical scholars of Greece and
Rome were shown to be in error by practical experience
stemming from increasing contacts with the whole of the
world and the new understanding of the place of planet
Earth within the universe, due to the impact of Copernicus
and Columbus. The authority of church dogma was
overthrown; it seemed to deny the real relationship
between man and God. This relationship was now seen as
personal; it worked through grace and was justified by
faith. The authority of temporal rulers, kings, who failed to
adhere to the newly revealed truth of the gospels, was not
binding to those who dissented from the religion of their

ruler. The authority of Protestants over social life reformed European convention. Believers had a duty to think, a warrant to interpret the world for themselves, guided by their personal conscience and experience of grace. The laity were no longer separate from the secondary to the religious and the clergy. The life of this present, secular world became more important to European thought, as did the understanding of its history.

The Reformation is dated from Martin Luther pinning his 95 theses to the cathedral door of Wuttenburg in 1517. It did not develop into a full rupture until the Diet of Worms in that fateful year of 1521. No sooner had Magellan brought a whole globe into European orbit than the world of Europe was split apart and vital questions concerning Europe's understanding of itself had to be answered afresh. Newness, change and the invention of progress as historical process in the present impressed themselves on European consciousness under the impact of the Reformation. However, these ideas were legitimated by the worldview of early Christianity, and the development of this worldview into a reformulated conception of human nature and civil society would have been impossible without the medieval gaze that *oculus mundi* turned on the New World.

Thus, there was no rupture in the application of medieval iconography and ideas to the peoples of the New World. The invention of the Other was a vital tool for European self-consciousness, whether influenced by Protestantism or the Counter-Reformation. Luther explicitly rejected Aristotle, who he thought was on his way to hell, in favour of St Augustine. Yet Augustine, too, shared an essentially Aristotelian notion of Otherness and barbarity.

When the unitary framework that united European self-consciousness was under threat, its need to redefine what was European laid even greater stress on the horrors without. While Europe bathed itself in blood with a savagery that almost surpassed its activities overseas, it is little wonder that the imagery of noble savages living in an earthly paradise of a Golden Age had immense potency, especially since these utopian idylls marked off Other People as the real barbarians.

The answer to where Columbus had gone soon crystallised as America, the New World. How, then, did one administer a new world, and what was the status of the new people it contained vis-a-vis Europeans? These questions were earnestly debated in Spain by special councils or *juntas* called by the monarchs. Contending viewpoints were expressed by canonical and civil lawyers, and by theologians, to resolve the legal framework for the disposal of rights over land and people under the control of Spain.

The debates employed familiar medieval categories of thought and argument and, as Padgen (1982) has shown, brought modern anthropology into existence. St Thomas Aquinas had systematised the medieval understanding of Aristotle and given two general categories of Otherness to Europe. The first was the invincibly ignorant, those who had heard the message of the gospel and refused through their incorrigibility to accept its message. This category consisted of the Muslims, Jews and other semites, and the Others who had been part of Europe's experience throughout its existence. The second category were the vincibly ignorant, those who, through no fault of their own, had never properly encountered the message of the Gospel, and hence could be evangelised and converted.

There was then a gradation of Otherness in which adherence to Christianity and tractability to Christian instruction was the distinguishing mark of what constituted fully humanised and civilised people. It was a quite explicit and persistent part of European consciousness that without Christianity not only was there no salvation but there was no full civil life, since there was no space between the definition of the norms of behaviour of humanity in general and the norms of Christian behaviour. Aquinas had speculated on the origin of civil life, but he left no doubt that it was through social character traits that basic human nature was demonstrated in the world.

This distinction was the focus of the Spanish debates about the peoples of the New World. The central theme in these debates did not come from within Spain, but was provided by the Scottish theologian and historian John Mair (Johannes Major) who was based at the College de Montaigu in Paris, a university with a tradition of not supporting the universal claims of popes or emperors. Mair, then, became the first in a long succession of Scottish intellectuals who indelibly marked the course of European thinking. The idea that John Mair took from Aristotle and included in his book of 1519 was that 'by nature, barbarians and slaves are the same'. The continuing debate must not be viewed purely in terms of narrow self-interest and political expediency, though these undoubtedly played an important role; it must be seen in terms of the exertions of *oculus mundi* to integrate and resolve the questions posed by its invention of a new world.

The first Spanish junta met in 1504 and concluded that Amerindians were vassals of the crown, who could dispose of them legitimately. The real challenge came in 1511 when the Dominican, Antonio de Monesinos traduced the citizens of Hispaniola for the 'cruel and terrible servitude' they imposed on the Amerindians. This charge struck at the roots of the ambiguity of Spanish claims to legitimate suzerainty over the New World. The Spaniards could cite the papal concession of rights over any lands they acquired. But this was shaky political and legal ground. There was no widespread acceptance that the Pope had the authority to dispose of such territory, especially at a time when papal authority was at its weakest and the popes themselves at their venal nadir.

Legally, too, it was a moot point. The legal framework of European thought was historical: it saw the papacy as an inheritance from the twin pillars of Christendom. The popes were the successors of St Peter with a lineal authority going back to Christ himself. And they were the spiritual encapsulation of Europe's descent from the Roman Empire from which came much of Europe's legal thinking.

So there were three categories of rights, which incorporated three categories of pagans. First, those who lived outside the church but on lands that had once been part of the Roman Empire and were thus reclaimable and within the dominion, the property of the church. The Spanish crown used such claims to legitimise its rights to land in North Africa, arguing that the Spanish were the successors of the Vandals who had occupied these areas in Roman times.

Second, there were areas and peoples in the world who were lawfully subject to a Christian prince. Such rule derived from the medieval conventions concerning conquest, taking land in a just war, or by treaty, when a local ruler acknowledged the overlordship of a Christian prince in the feudal manner. This was the model employed by the Portuguese in the East Indies.

The third category contained the true infidels, people of lands that were neither subject to legitimate Christian rule according to the second category nor had ever been within the bounds of the Roman world. The people of this third category, the category that included the Amerindians, were not within the framework of Christian rule either *de jure* or *de facto*. They were a problem, one that Columbus had helped to create by his reports of the pacific nature of the inhabitants of the New World and their tractability to Christian instruction. This brings us back to the papal concessions, which had efficacy only if their terms were fulfilled, and these insisted on the Christianisation of the Amerindians without inflicting 'dangers or hardships' upon them.

The institution at the centre of the debate that questioned the right of the Spanish crown to sovereignty over the New World was the *encomienda*. This is no abstruse argument, for the *encomienda* is part of the social formation of Latin America to this day, the backdrop of every land reform movement that has ever taken place and foundered inconclusively. The *encomienda* is the allocation of so many head of people to an *encomiendero*, who thereby acquires a servile and cheap labour force. The problem was that if the territory, the physical space of the New World, actually belonged to Spain by papal donation, the crown could not make war against its own vassals, the inhabitants of the New World. Such a war would not be just, nor could the crown wilfully enslave the people.

If the right of the Pope to dispose of lands that had never been part of the Roman world was questioned, as of course it was by other European monarchs anxious to acquire territory for themselves in the New World, some other means of justifying Spanish sovereignty had to be elaborated, and it was here that the idea of the barbarian as a natural slave became crucial. People were barbarians because of flaws in their reason, and this was established by the manner and mores of their social life. It was a behavioural fact that could be observed. Such natural barbarians could not have sufficient reason to be said to have full possession of dominion or rights over their land and property.

Also, by their nature, such people were natural slaves, able to apprehend the reason of others and follow commands. They were also naturally dependent. Since such people had no true dominion over their land or their persons, the former could be acquired legitimately by the first Christian monarch to come across this fortuitous space. Indeed, it was worthy and permissible for the Spanish crown to enslave such natural slaves, since their proximity to civilised Christians would assist their rise out of what might, under tutelage, be a treatable condition, and thus their enslavement would be to their benefit.

If this argument sounds familiar to the one used in the debate on black slavery that ran throughout European annals until the nineteenth century, it is hardly surprising, for it is indeed the same. The only difference is that there had never been any doubt about the rightness of enslaving the blacks since this could be substantiated neatly within the biblical context: it was Noah's curse on the descendants of Ham, the negro race, to be hewers of wood and drawers of water. It was then, the ambiguity of the status of the Amerindians, the difficulty in giving them an unequivocal biblical genealogy, that required elaborate definition, and focused European thinking on the implications of barbarism as natural slavery. As we have seen, the consistent tenor of the reports that came back from the New World expressed the social life of the Amerindian as the negative of European norms of civil life. These reports were therefore the substance of the legal argument about whether or not the people could be enslaved. They were also adjudged against the concept of natural law, a law implicit in humanity by its common divine creation. To have social behaviour that was inimical to natural law was to define oneself as a barbarian. This was a completely circular argument. The only way to be within the confines of natural law in the ultimate analysis was to be a Christian, since there was no conception of these laws that was not simultaneously a definition of Christian life.

When people back in Europe read Vespucci's *Novus Mundi*, for instance, they learnt that its inhabitants, 'have no laws or faith and live according to nature'. However, this did not mean they lived according to natural law, for animals also lived according to nature. It meant that the peoples of the New World lived entirely contrary to natural law. Vespucci went on to demonstrate this by stating that

> they have no private property because everything is common, they have no boundaries of kingdoms and provinces, no king ... They obey nobody, each is lord to himself .. [They have] no justice and no gratitude ... They are a very prolific people but have no heirs ...

And, of course, they were also consistently cannibals, again in utter violation of natural law. All these 'objective' tests confirmed their status as barbarians and led the Europeans back to the argument that such people could be enslaved.

The debate in Europe over the status of the Amerindian was not all one-way traffic. It brought to the forefront more sharply defined concepts of the Other and Otherness, but also inspired counter-arguments that denied the status of the Amerindians as natural slaves. There were those who denied the full humanity of the Amerindians, regarding them as part of the old category of *similitudines hominis*, hominid in appearance but between man and beast in the great chain of being that was a hierarchical ordering of all creation, a convention of the medieval outlook.

Others, notably Francisco de Vitoria (1492-1546) of the School of Salamanca, argued persistently against categorising the Amerindians as natural slaves. They were true humans, with reason, who were therefore in possession of dominion over their land and property and could only be enslaved according to the medieval conventions of being deemed inimical to Christ by resisting the preaching of the gospel.

It was this train of thought that led to the full development of the *requerimiento*, the declaration the conquistadores were required to declaim before an uncomprehending people, announcing the arrival of the Spanish and their intention to preach the gospels. Following the declaration the slightest sign of resistance would categorise the Amerindian as inimical to Christ, fit to be dispossessed of land and person.

De Vitoria had no problems with slavery as such. He expressed the uniform European view of the matter when he wrote: 'if they [the Africans] are treated humanely it is better for them to be slaves among Christians than free in their own lands, for it is the greatest good fortune to become a Christian.' But the ambiguity of the Amerindians had to be resolved otherwise, for these people were in their own land and free, even if they were not fortunate enough to be Christians. For this, de Vitoria went on to advance a different argument. He accepted that while the Amerindians might appear to be 'very little different from brute animals who are incapable of ruling themselves' they nevertheless had 'a certain rational order in their affairs'. The deficiency in the rationality of the Amerindians, then, was not inherent in their nature but the fault of their 'poor and barbarous education'.

In other words, the peoples of the New World were not natural slaves but natural children, heirs to the true reason once they had been properly educated and had grown up. Their cultural condition, based on their faulty education, made them incapable of fully rational behaviour and this warranted the Spanish crown's right to hold them and their lands in tutelage, until they reached the age of reason.

When Kipling, centuries later, summed up the white man's burden as nurturing the savage who was half devil and half child he was merely restating the basic concept of European colonialism, in its most favourable and humane version. The demonic part of the equation always existed in the medieval framework, as we have seen, and had much greater prominence in the Protestant response to barbarism, derived from the far greater Protestant reliance on reason as the basic human characteristic and on the reliability of the tools of reason to uncover the demonic imitations Satan used to mock the Christian world.

Natural children could be subject to *ecomienda* so long as this institution rested on regarding the *encomiendado* as being exercised on 'free' people who retained their freedom in a legal sense and did not become true slaves. The proviso was that the *encomiendero* should undertake to provide his dependents with Christian education and a minimal wage.

This became the full form and fictive usage of the encomienda. In practice it was close to the full, legal slavery that existed side by side with it in Spanish territory. However 'free' the *encomienda* might be as a legal nicety, the Amerindians could not freely move from one place to another and were tied to their master. As for the actual treatment and instruction they received from the conquistadores and settlers, the evasions and the non-observances were summed up in the phrase '*Obedezco pero no cumplo*', – 'I obey but I do not fulfil.'

The debate on the barbarian honed the tools of medieval thought afresh for a colonial encounter that had not been part of medieval experience. All the reports from around the globe constructed a servile array of Others and unfolded a new consciousness of the European self. In this process it was not merely the 'Them' who were defined but also the European 'Us'.

The corollary of the natural slave or the natural child was the existence of the natural master and the natural teacher representing an innately superior, Christian, way of life. Medieval Europe had entertained no doubt about the pre-eminence of Christianity but had a deep perplexity about why it failed to deliver mastery in the world. The ubiquitous medieval theme was the Crusade, which embroidered and wrestled with this central problem. Why, six centuries after Christ had walked on earth, had died to redeem all mankind and had established the only way to salvation and full human existence, had another Prophet arisen in Arabia? Why had the heresy of Islam spread so rapidly and acquired such worldly success that it threatened and dominated Europe? In its dependence upon Muslim civilisation, source not merely of goods but also of knowledge and techniques, medieval Christianity had a sense not of triumphant superiority but of gnawing self-doubt.

Only after these 29 years of rapid expansion from 1492 to 1521, designed to out-manoeuvre Muslim dominance, did the conditions exist for Christian self-confidence to re-emerge. The triumphalism of the worldview that constructed Europe found new meaning when it was embodied and symbolised by the domination of such vast lands and so many peoples all around the globe. The natural master could only be fashioned as a European when the gaze of *oculus mundi* was turned across the Atlantic to the New World whose possession marked off this new era from all its predecessors. The torch of civilisation was moving westward, from Greece to Rome and to the Atlantic litoral, or from Jerusalem to Rome and to the Atlantic seaboard. So much was expressed by Machiavelli, and later by Vico, Herder and Hegel.

The anthropology of Otherness that was fashioned to include the New World in the universal framework of European understanding could become a new global convention that would now envelop and change Europe's relations with even those continents that had been known within the medieval convention – Africa and Asia.

The cultural conditions of the people of the New World and their deviations from Christian norms were frequently read off against existing models of barbarity contained in the medieval and classical storehouse. The Amerindians were like Ethiopians (a term that could be applied to anyone from Abyssinia to India), or Thracians or Scythians. There was no conception that these peoples who had existed in ancient times might have been subject to history and change.

There were no historical imaginations either, as the iconography of history and travel writing of the medieval period makes abundantly clear. To examine the illustrations of the *Lives de Merveilles*, a fourteenth-century collection of travel writings concluding Mandeville, Marco Polo and Friar Odoric, is to find Indian elephants whose howdahs are modelled on medieval ships or battlements, and where the procession of the Great Khan looks like an illustration of a European royal progress. Other times, other places and Other Peoples were depicted according to familiar imagery. When Holinshed's *Chronicles* were published in 1577 they included an illustration of the ancient British queen Boadicea confronting the Roman legions. Boadicea is the very image of Queen Elizabeth I and the Roman legions are conventional soldiers of the Elizabethan period.

However, when Thomas Harriot published his *A Brief and True Account of the New Found Land of Virginia* in 1588 it was illustrated by the artist John White. White's beautiful and meticulous drawings, now in the British Museum, may have owed a great deal to classical proportion but they also showed a new attention to the ethnography of the people of America, their dress, homes, tools and agricultural economy. When Harriot's and White's work was republished in 1592 in part one of *America* by Johannes de Bry it included an appendix entitled 'Some pictures of the Pictes which in the old tyme dyd habite one part of the great Britainne'. The ancient Britons, Rome's barbarians, were now depicted as Amerindians. Europe had acquired a new mental picture of peoples of the past. The antiquarians of Europe were able to acquire a new body of information and imagery to inform the notion of the original condition of mankind. The process of inventing the primitive had begun, and leapt direct from the newness of the New World. Employing what Margaret T. Hodgen called 'old and convivial ideas', the medieval and classical intellectual inheritance, the European mind began to fashion a new sense of history as a progress of civilisation from its primal, original condition to the present day, where Europe, instead of being beholden to other civilisations, could see itself as the culmination of all civilisations.

In this progress extant peoples of the earth who were now within the dominion of Europe became evidence of stages through which European civilisation had passed on its upward journey. The question that would fascinate and redefine the European self-image was phrased anew in the post-Columbian era by Michel de Montaigne (1533-1592), who had plenty of opportunity to observe Amerindians imported to France to entertain at carnival sideshows. The question appears, appropriately, in his essay *On the Cannibals*: 'to what was that partition into civil and uncivil to be ascribed?' The question goes on being asked in various forms down through the years in Europe. It is still being asked today in the development debate: why did industrialisation, the scientific and industrial revolutions, happen in Europe and nowhere else?

Fitting the people of the New World into the biblical

framework of explanation was part of the search for an answer to this sort of question and for a unitary understanding of the universal existence of mankind. Civilisation was interchangeable with the term 'culture' and, as the historian of anthropology George Stocking Jr has pointed out, both were used in the singular until the late nineteenth century.

One could have different ideas about what happened to mankind after the fall from grace and expulsion from Eden. There could have been a primal innocence from which man had risen under the hand of providence, or a degeneration into barbarism by those who did not fall into the orbit or refused the guidance of providence. Those earliest reports of the 'earthly Paradise' provided by Columbus and Vespucci and so many others contained a new way to thinking about such issues. The ancient Greek formula of the three ages, the Gold, Bronze and Iron, ceased to be in a link between mythic and modern time and became a concept of historical time.

The extant and real people of the world that Europe was busy inventing all around the globe, by the application of Christian terms and conventions to their cultural life, were being employed simultaneously to create a new sense of the past. The Other was not merely removed from Europe by being a savage or a barbarian who lived differently outside the church or Christian confession. All Others, thanks to the newness of America, were sundered by being people of a past age that Europe had transcended. Other people had remained static, they stayed where Europe had been in its history, while Europe had progressed spiritually, intellectually and physically beyond the confines of the ancient world.

However crude it may sound, the uniform offer Europe made to Other Peoples in its great explosive movement around the globe was to choose between enslavement or conversion. This much was contained in the philosophy of the papal bulls that legitimated the process. We have seen how enslavement was justified by conceptualising the barbarian as being by nature dependent on the natural master. Conversion was the tool for teaching the arts and uses of civilisation.

The crowns of Spain and Portugal were the most Catholic of monarchs. The crowns' privileges, granted by the popes, made them administrators of both the temporal and spiritual affairs in their new possessions. The church was under their control, and the appointment of its personnel in the new lands was a royal perogative. For the monarchs, the church in these territories had explicit political functions. Conversion was understood by monarchs and by the missionaries they despatched as a means of separating the pagans from their former condition and as an induction into the Christian worldview, which was coterminus with the European way of life. As Axtell (1981) put it: 'To convert the Indians of America was to replace their native characters by substituting predictable European modes of thinking and feeling for unpredictable native ones.' The process was not confined to America; its scope was global.

The assimilation of Other people to the manners and mores of Europe was no instant transformation. It did not put the new Christians on a par with their masters. It involved changes in habits, dress, food, marriage customs, family connections, often abode, language and political affiliation, as the means of getting civilised. It was a process of transformation intimately connected with the debates on enslavement, as is revealed by the comment of Sir William Johnson, an English settler in North America.

Johnson explained that it was necessary to 'civilize the savages before they can be converted to Christianity' and that 'in order to make them Christians, they must first be made Men'. The natural slave and the natural child was a conditional man; they could not be left in their state of nature, acting contrary to natural law. That was an offence to the Christian conscience. Once that had been changed, they could be given, or would be ready to receive, the true benefit of civilisation and its culmination, Christianity.

But it would only make them second-class citizens. Christianity remained a European cultural product, whose evaluation and definition remained in the hands of the master. In reality, the masters perennially deferred the passing-out examination. As the missionaries were constantly complaining, these new Christians were often acquired by brute force, at the point of a sword, improperly educated in their new faith and its social mores; and there were never enough missionaries anyway to attend to the work of evangelisation, not least since the priests who did arrive in the dominions were too busy undertaking the commercial exploitation of the new territories to attend to harvesting souls.

As Boxer (1991) points out, the Portuguese were loathe to appoint indigenous Christians to positions in the church in order to overcome the missionary problem either in India or in Africa. This held true despite occasional notable exceptions. But conversion did create a tractable hinterland for the Portuguese outposts and Spanish territory. The Laws of Burgos of 1513 showed the Spanish approach to conversion in the New World. It agreed to the herding of Amerindians away from their former homes because inconstant Christians were prone to flee to the jungle. This was a perennial colonial complaint. There was a constant suspicion among the colonisers that the Amerindians' sole aim in life was to have the freedom to do with themselves exactly as they pleased.

This was a freedom the post-Columbian world could not afford. It produced in the New World the most remarkable of all circular movements. To aid the process of conversion by distancing the Amerindians from the brutalities of the settlers some Catholic orders began to set up new communities. The first such example was instituted by one Vasco de Quiroga with his village hospitals in Sante Fe, Mexico. Quiroga was firmly against slavery, that is, he was a staunch supporter of *encomienda*. In his *Informacion en Derecho* of 1535 he gave comprehensive arguments for the indigenous peoples' lack of rights in their own land. These people could be herded away from their former abodes and distributed into *encomienda* because they did not have rights of dominion, which belonged only to those 'who at least know and observe the natural law, do not worship many gods, and have a king and an ordered politic life'. In the Americas, instead, its people were living 'in tyranny of themselves as barbarous and cruel persons, in ignorance of things and of the good and politic life', which went a long way to explain how they could be so oblivious of the mechanisms of the natural world as to allow themselves to be easily overrun by the Spaniards.

Among such peoples as the Aztec and the Inca there had been no true politics; only tyrants who were wor- shipped 'not as a human being among free people but as a god among captive, oppressed and servile people'. They were ripe for conversion under supervision, which was best undertaken in special communities where they could be led to a full Christian life. The Jesuits later adopted this model. Thus, when they separated the Amerindians from the rapacious Spanish settlers, it did not mean giving them the liberty to do with themselves exactly as they pleased.

It seems likely that Quiroga was influenced in establishing his village hospitals by a book in the possession of his superior, the first Archbishop of Mexico, Juan de Zumarraga. The book was Thomas More's *Utopia* which, as we have seen, was itself based on Vespucci's *Novus Mundi*, and inspired by Iambolous! More's classic condemnation of the material conditions of European civil life, what one might term the tyranny of property, would have been heresy had he rooted his ideas in examples drawn from European history. Property, dominion, the crucial question of the New World, was understood by Europe as an essential feature of civil life, and property relations as something that could arise only in true civil society.

Yet Christian movements based on the idea of holding all property in common and living in pacific community had been a persistent part of medieval experience. They included the Cathar heresy that had prompted an internal Crusade in Europe, and the Waldensian heresy. These were familiar unmentionables. To argue for the amendment of property relations in Europe, More used the visionary possibilities of information brought back from America by Ralph Hythlodacus, shipwrecked while accompanying Amerigo Vespucci to the New World.

Ideas from the New World also assisted and made possible the devising of new strategies to promote individual liberty in Europe. The idea of man's primal condition and the stages of human progress were informed by contact with Other Peoples. Both ideas played a crucial part in structuring European political debate for centuries. It is there in Hobbes ('the war of all against all'), in Rousseau (the liberty of the noble savage as understood in the Tahitian century), and in Karl Marx. It is there in the romantic movement that crystallised the concepts of nationalism and racism.

Every development in Europe's relationship with its own self involved a new relationship with, and understanding of, its past. And this past was composed of interpretations of the diversity and condition of the peoples Europe now controlled and administered around the globe. But when these ideas arrived in the New World and were practised on the indigenous people the processes they engineered turned out to have a slightly different meaning with, of course, frightful consequences.

The idea that wild men must be tamed and civilised or, if not, exterminated, was not unique to the Spanish (Roman Catholic) experience of South America. It was also to be found at the root of the Protestant takeover of North America. The symbols of both conquests were the same: Christianity's mandate with regard to the savagery of the Amerindians.

The principal anxiety of North America's white republican leaders, after they had cut themselves off from the King of England was the relationship between virtue, which they saw as being synonymous with self-control, and good government. Republican ideology rooted in the Protestant ethic was promoted by intellectual and political leaders as a strategy to domesticate and discipline the emotional part of themselves and to set themselves apart even further from the blacks and Indians, both of these groups being associated with the 'instinctual life'. In any event, it was quite obvious to white settlers that both blacks and Indians were not associated with virtue.

Likewise, the Indians were seen as creatures of passion, wild and primitive, lacking the control and the inclination to labour that whites believed were necessary if men were to be civilised. One extreme view described them as 'animals, vulgarly called Indians'. Like Shakespeare's Caliban, they were not masters of their natural life. They could not therefore be republicans. To be a republican, reason must be in command. Whites were naturally associated with rationality, or the mind, whereas people of colour were associated with the body. Thus, just as mind was in authority over the other parts of the self, so whites were raised above blacks and Indians. Jefferson had two views of the Indian: he could be civilised and assimilated or he could be removed, possibly exterminated. This view would repeat itself time and again. For Jefferson, progress meant advance from savagery to pastoral and then urban civilisation, from past to present: the Indian was identified with nature, with the past, and the past had to be dominated.

A diversified society with whites, blacks and Indians was a danger to a republican society therefore, because it would include groups who lived the instinctual life close to nature. Black intelligence was according to Jefferson, inferior, and Indian intelligence was underdeveloped. It followed then, that both lacked possibilities or self-control that civilised men must have. The black, in fact, seemed unable to develop beyond childhood. 'The same power that has given him a black skin with less weight in volume of brain has given us a white skin, with greater volume of brain and intellect', wrote one writer. Thus, whites saw the black 'child/savage' as the antithesis of their own self-image and of what they valued, lacking 'incentive to industry', moral restraint, the principle of accumulation and control over the animal part of man. 'What good man would prefer a country covered with forests and ranged by a few thousand savages to our extensive Republic, studded with cities, towns and prosperous farms ... filled with all the blessings of liberty, civilization, and religion?' Children of the forests, the Indians, did not cultivate the land. How could they make claims on tracts on which they had neither dwelt nor made improvements?

The government, Jefferson told Andrew Jackson in 1803, must keep agents among the Indians to lead them to agriculture and to advise them to sell their 'useless' extensive forests in order to obtain money and purchase clothes and comforts from federal trading houses. They would, naturally, be subject to extermination if they did not behave.

Later, the whites professed to be distressed that the Indians had been with them for two centuries and yet showed no improvement:

Like the bear, and deer, and buffalo of his own forests, an Indian lives as his father lived, and dies as his father died. He never attempts to imitate the arts of his civilized neighbours. His life passes away in a succession of listless indolence, and of vigorous exertion to provide for his animal wants, or to gratify his baleful passions. Efforts .... have not been wanting to teach and reclaim him. But he is perhaps destined to disappear with the forests ...

Neither could the forests themselves be abandoned to

hopeless sterility but must give way to the march of civilisation and improvement. If something had no utility, it could be extinguished. Jefferson wrote:

> The laws [of Virginia] have also descended to the preservation and improvement of the races of useful animals, such as horses, cattle, deer; to the extirpation of those which are noxious, as wolves, squirrels, crows, blackbirds; and to the guarding of our citizens against infectious disorders, by obliging suspected vessels coming into the state, to perform quaratine, and by regulating the conduct of persons having such disorders within the state.

'Races' of 'useful' animals must be improved, noxious ones extirpated. The new nation had to be isolated from diseases of any sort. Everything threatening to republican society had to be purged.

Tocqueville writes about how whites, in their expansion westward, were able to deprive Indians of their rights and to exterminate them 'with singular felicity, tranquillity, legally, philanthropically, without shedding blood, and without violating a single great principle of morality in the eyes of the world.' This was untrue, of course, and Tocqueville was not witness to the greatest purges and holocausts that occurred.

During the age of Andrew Jackson, US President from 1829, some 7,000 Indians were removed from their homes in the south and driven west of the Mississippi river. As a result of violence, disease, starvation, dangerous travel conditions and harsh winter weather almost one-third of the southern Indians died. An important objective of Jackson's removal policy was to make the lands of the so-called 'five civilised nations' available to white settlers. The 'five civilised nations' – the Cherokee, Creeks,

Choctaws, Chickasaws and Seminoles – acquired their sobriquet from their willingness to accommodate the manners and accoutrements of white civilisation. Where the Americans found the Indian unchanging, the Indians found white civilisation consistently duplicitous. By 1844, the south had become a white man's country.

Following the ratification of the fraudulent Treaty of New Echota towards the end of the eighteenth century, thousands of white intruders moved into Cherokee territory, seizing farms and cultivating lands, and forcing out and often murdering the inhabitants. Still the Cherokee refused to recognise the treaty and leave their territory; finally, in 1838, the federal government ordered the army to round up 15,000 of them. Placed in detention camps and then marched west beyond the Mississippi in the dead of winter, more than 4,000 Cherokees died on the Trail of Tears.

In the early nineteenth century, US Senator Thomas Hart Benton (see Welsh, 1890, and Gabriel, 1929) saw no particular difficulty in resuming the vocabulary and design of Columbus: the children of Adam were completing their circumambulation of the globe by marching across America from the east coast to the west to the Pacific Ocean 'in sight of the eastern shore of that Asia in which their first parents were originally planted'.

As Benton explained to Congress in 1846, the arrival of the white race on the west coast would benefit mankind. On the other side was the yellow race which 'must receive an impression from the superior race whenever they come into contact'. Benton claimed that the white race alone had received the divine command to subdue and replenish the earth, 'for it was the only race which searched for new and

distant lands. As they made their restless movements from
western Asia they developed religion, art, science, destroy-
ing savagery and savages as they advanced civilization'.
About the disappearance of the Indians from the Atlantic
coast, he noted that one could not murmur against what
appears to be the effect of divine law. The white race was to
take the ascendant and elevate and improve the yellow race
from its torpidity.

After the Mexican–US war, with Mexico subdued, it
was more than ever apparent that 'there are some nations
that have a doom upon them ... The nation that makes no
onward progress ... that wastes its treasures wantonly –
that cherishes not its resources – such a nation will burn
out ... will become the easy prey of the more adventurous
enemy'.

Thereafter, American expansion set itself 'on the road
to India,' ousting the Spanish from the Philippines, and
began to penetrate the markets of Asia. The purveyors of
American aggression and destructiveness preached the
gospel of the strenuous life. The takeover of the Far East
would result from decadent conditions there and the lack
of Asian power to resist encroachments from a more
virile nation. It was civilised men who required more
territory. Incompetent races were destined to be
destroyed; inferior ones had fallen back and disappeared
before the persistent impact of the superior.

No one had a natural right to land: that right de-
pended upon physical fitness. Only those who utilised the
land, made certain its resources were not left idle, were
entitled to it. Lands inhabited by Indians were lying
waste, which contravened the very purpose of human life.
Civilised men would now control the areas of the world

which still remained in the possession of savages, and would use the land and its resources for the general good of the world. The descendants of Columbus would use the institutions of colonialism and imperialism to raise the human quality of all men everywhere.

This latest Columbian design was thus directed to the domination of the undeveloped areas. This time, the lands contained primitive Filipinos and savage Chinese. America would regenerate the stationary and barbarous Chinese, who were still in their childhood. Savagery, whether in America or Asia, must yield to civilisation. The profession of war had thus become the highest moral expression of American asceticism. Nothing had changed from the days in which Columbus had seen the Arawak and dreamed of enslaving them for their own good. The only difference was that the destructiveness of the Anglo-Saxon, the inheritor of the Columbus legacy, had now become global. It had no destination pending, now, other than its own, final destruction.

Thus, 500 years on, Christopher Columbus remains in resplendent, and seemingly unchallenged, command: a plethora of global institutions busy themselves in continuing and deepening his search for the fabled Indies. He looked for gold and spices; they look for profits and for change. Both are related to the emptiness within and to the tastelessness of ordinary life without. The fundamental question, why he had to leave his shores and impose himself on the rest of humankind, need no longer remain unanswered. To still the cauldron of activity, however, would expose the pointlessness of the effort in all its dimensions. In the meantime, development has replaced the encomienda *within* the South.

4 THE POST-COLUMBIAN EPOCH

EUROPE'S IMPOSITION OF ITSELF on the New World unleashed a myriad cultural and psychological forces, many of them not yet fully manifest even after 500 years. We have tried to identify some of them here. Three of these forces have become crucial in a colonial and post-colonial world where European culture has been globalised and made absolute. Together these forces have turned Christopher Columbus into a cultural presence in every civilisation. He is no longer simply out there in history, a cultural hero of the West to be applauded, criticised or even jettisoned in the five-hundredth year of his grand success. He has to be confronted within, even by those who have apparently escaped the West's loving embrace and who have had nothing to do with the European repertoire Columbus carried with him to the New World. We shall look again at these three issues as a prelude to our concluding remarks. The first is represented by those who wished to replace the native character of the American Indians with, in Axtell's words (1981), 'European modes of thinking and feeling' in order to get rid of their 'unpredictable native modes'. Half-way round the world, thousands of miles away, Lord Macaulay (1800-59) was to attempt a similar substitution in colonial India, the original destination for Columbus's voyage.

The native modes that were found 'unpredictable', and therefore difficult to bring under control or surveillance, included both culture and human nature. Both had to be engineered to produce institutions and personalities that would be familiar to Europe and thus predictable and controllable. Once remoulded, such natives were to remain, according to Macaulay, natives in their looks alone; they were to become European in their manners, in their habits of mind and in their impulses. This social engineering has now become the legitimate goal of every repressive not-Western regime operating within the European concept of the nation-state, development and scientific rationality. State formation, development and modernisation in general have now become the routine excuses for the abridgement of civil liberties and for state violence, and naturally found enthusiastic supporters among the Western nation-states.

In fact, such regimes have gone one better. While in pre-modern Europe the responsibility of the nation-state remained confined largely to issues concerning national security and economic prosperity, in the savage world (today's Third World), the nation-state has, in addition, taken on the white man's burden: to drag entire populations out of their 'superstitious', 'irrational', 'unscientific', and 'retrogressive' ways of life into the ways of the modern West.

Second, long before the likes of H. G. Wells popularised the concept of time travel, and long before particle physics popularised the concept of the inter-translatability of space and time in nature, the New World allowed Europe a new cultural play of its own manufactured out of the Others' pasts, presents and futures. In this play, Europe's past was systematically represented as the present of the not-Western world. What Europe and the rest of the modern West had once been during their pre-modern incarnations, now only the Other was reportedly backward enough to remain mired in. The equation between the savage and the child was established as the final justification for the civilising mission of colonial and post-colonial domination.

Likewise, Europe's present was rewritten as the future of the Others. What the West was now, according to the new theory of progress, the Other could become in the future, provided they were rational and mature enough to know their own good and internalise Western values and conventions. The fact that parts of the Other were capable of showing enough 'maturity' to internalise the West in its entirety gave further confidence to the carriers of the culture of Christopher Columbus.

In both forms of time travel the West has remained the measure of everything valuable, culturally and psychologically – the concerned expert to the rest of the world in the latter's sickness. The West presumably understands the rest of the world better than the rest themselves, for the rest only live in their present, whereas the West has lived in that present (it being the West's past) and transcended it; the West knows the Other's future better than the Other itself does, for the Other has to still enter that future, whereas the West is at this moment living out that future.

Chroniclers of the New World characterised the Amerindians as being subject to the 'tyranny of themselves'. The logic of that reading of the savage permeates all aspects of the West's dealings with the rest of the world, as well as the dealings of Westernised Third World elites with their own people. The savage as a natural child and the savage as a natural slave are imageries that have, over the last 200 years, acquired even greater potency and applicability than they possessed in fifteenth-century Europe with the institution of the *encomienda*. William Johnson claimed, the reader may remember, that to civilise savages one had to first Christianise them, but to Christianise them one had first to turn them into 'men'. That project continues with as much enthusiasm today under the reportedly benign tutelage of the northern states and corporate structures, including the multilateral development banks, as under the numerous southern despots.

Finally, we have pointed out that the terms 'civilisation' and 'culture' were always used in the singular till the nineteenth century. The idea of 'choseness' has systematically subverted and marginalised all modes of dissent that have not conformed to the concept of dissent permitted at the centre of the global culture. Nothing has ensured the stability of the present global order, organised around Europe's *oculus mundi*, more faithfully than this management of dissent. As the citadels of in-house dissent have collapsed one after another in the northern theatre (the Marxist-Leninist project being last in the series), the mainstream global culture has not only acquired a greater sense of permanence and omnipotence, but it has become more dismissive of the dissent that has not been articulated in the language of the mainstream – dissent that looks to the West. All non-Western forms of dissent are deemed chaotic, uncontrollable, childish, disorganised and irrational.

Christopher Columbus, then, seems finally to have triumphed. After 500 years of marauding vandalism and colonialism, he has arranged through 200 years of education and modernisation to clone himself within the savage world. Probably he does not have to be at the centre of the world stage any more. He might willingly allow himself to be the butt of criticism, wit and sarcasm the world over, even among his erstwhile admirers. The West may not even have to keep him alive as symbol of victory or confident self-criticism, for the rest of the world can accomplish this on its own.

Yet, everything considered, the non-Western world cannot disown its cultural self entirely, even it wants to do so. Its version of the *oculus mundi* cannot be other than inauthentic and occasionally comic. In that inauthenticity and comicality there is always another play that is possible – there is always the possibility of a failure to live up to the expectations of the West. The play and the failure offer a small way out for the non-West from an otherwise totalising situation. In many southern societies everyday forms of dissent and resistance thwart the process of modernisation and provide these societies with a degree of individuality and link with their history. The persistence of community life and traditions in the South, is in total defiance of the global forces of homogenisation.

Neither the play nor the escape route is available to the European mind. Nor is either available to those strands of dissent within it that seek today to disown the Columbian world image and heritage. The repression of the Other within the West is much more complete. The near total breakdown of community life, brought about by massifica-tion, the successful atomisation of the individual, and the full-scale marketisation of a kind that ultimately colours all dissent and the defiance of dominant social trends, all render even the Western intellectual tradition an almost foolproof monocultural strain. The dissenting civilisational streams within the West may have to survive outside the West – in the surviving cultural pluralities of the Other and, strangely enough, perhaps even in the acquired or

imported biculturality of those exposed to the West. For, if
the West has had a theory of the Other, that Other too has
now developed its own theories of the West.

The events of 1492, therefore, cannot be the concern of
Europe alone, nor do they comprise simply a non-Western
predicament. They constitute a shared memory, tragic, but,
to the extent it is shared, a memory that could serve as a
base line for pluralising and humanising our futures. Only
when this possibility is explored, its implications honestly
acknowledged, can we recover the lost reality of all the
world's peoples; only then can we uncover what has been
invisible in the common knowledge pool around the globe.

The point of release requires us to go back to 1492, in a
sense, and to recover the underside of the worldview that
Europe established centre-stage. Within Columbus's generation that same worldview went on to encompass the whole
globe. From 1492 to the 1990s we are dealing not with
change, rupture and difference but rather with suppression,
amnesia and deliberate avoidance of realities, cultural as
well as psychological. We are dealing with the deformed
sight of a blinded eye.

The eye of the West, the civilisation that arose by
straddling the Atlantic space opened up by Columbus, was
blind when it turned to observe what was not European or
Western. When it observed the Other, *oculus mundi* was
blinded, paradoxically, by its own perceptions and pre-
visions. It not merely helped falsify the Other, but in fact
invented it out of Europe's own inner demons – Europe's
fears, anxieties and disowned self.

Once the concept of the Other that already existed in
the European imagination acquired flesh, Europe proceeded to administer and interact with the Others as if they

were nothing other than what it perceived. The vast diversity of peoples around the world were lumped together for all practical purposes in one, gigantic category of Otherness. The distinctness of a particular Other was lost in the generality shared with all Others, that of being different and sundered from the West. This distinctiveness was left for the experts or professionals to debate.

British administration in India, for instance, was shaped by antiquarian studies rooted in the conventions of Otherness. The form of the British Raj retained its intellectual debt to the old medieval categories, and to the likes of James Mill who studied and speculated by means of these ideas. It proceeded to deal with real Indians as if they were part of a static, inflexible tradition, a tradition that could have no autonomous impulse to change. All that could cause or create change had to belong to the West, not to the living traditions of the people who inhabited the landmass called India.

This conception of the nature of tradition lives on within India and within practically all non-Western societies. It has been diffused into the Other's concepts of self by the most enduring legacy of 1492, the colonisation of the self, the implanting of Columbus within. It is implicit in the modern education apparatus, the modern apparatus of the state, the axioms that are encoded with and products of ideas of Otherness. Independent nation-states of the non-Western world now hunger after this imported education in order to acquire 'mastery' over their own problems and to imbibe deeper ignorance of their autonomous past. The desire to acquire 'good and useful' knowledge with which to change their circumstances, requires that the Others must be unknown to themselves.

In the modern world, thus, the Others have now been confronted by a dual incomprehensibility: the difference between the West and their actual self; the difference between their actual self and the invented self Europe gave them. The dual battle to overturn colonial imposition, with its political and social controls, and the idea of the Other that legitimated and sustained the control, has dislocated all Other civilisations within themselves.

The real triumph of the blinded gaze of *oculus mundi* is that even today all negotiation with Western civilisation must be carried out through the West's conventions. In order to secure amendment or concession, real people have to act either as if they were the Other invented by Europe or as if they had become part of the West. So complete is this triumph that today the Other, too, negotiates with its real self through the conventions of Western civilisation.

Thus the future allows the Others the same two false choices that Columbus first proffered them in 1492: enslavement or conversion. The only progress we have made in 500 years is that today the Others have the option either of an 'authenticity' constructed by the dominant, or living on as a parody of their former selves. Nothing more is permissible or possible within the current debate on the new world order because it remains within the confines of the Columbian politics of consciousness.

In 1492 *oculus mundi* turned the blind gaze of Europe's history to the unknown and made it knowable by enforcing a great lie. In the 1990s all histories are corrupted by that lie. The task we face is not that of being nice to Amerindians, a people for whom we do not even have a name, apart from the one authored by the great lie. Nor is the task to be nasty to Christopher Columbus and all he stands for – for that scapegoating has been given to us as an easy option and as a compensation for conformity in other crucial sectors of life.

The task is to render the West's *oculus mundi*, this eye of the world, visible in all its deformation so that people everywhere can see themselves clearly once again. The European landfall in the Americas is the starting point of a debate in which all the peoples of the world, willy-nilly, now find their identity. It is the primal moment of a new and unprecendented global system of power and knowledge that renders plurality, diversity and multicultural dialogue, conversation and exchange a practically insurmountable enterprise in today's world. The dilemma confronts the Muslin, the Hindu, the Chinese and the Japanese, the Amerindian and the European, as well as the citizen of the United States of America.

The 1990s call for a simple vote for or against Columbus, for Columbus the hero or against Columbus the villain, is in effect a validation of the constitution of the great lie without questioning the perversion of reality it authors. But the discovery that is yet to be made 500 years on is how little we can know about ourselves, whoever we are, because of the triumph of ignorance Columbus made possible. All questions, all the terms of the debate about human nature and human diversity, its causes and effects, its consequences and implications, reach back to the events of 12 October 1492. That watershed established not only what it is to be modern, but what it is to be Other, not European, distinct from the West.

Thus a condemnation of Columbus is insufficient to give the Other, in all its diversity, an autonomous existence in the modern world. Nor can it liberate the West to engage in a new way with the Other. Many times over the last 500 years the Columbian legacy has been reformulated to suppress and distance uncomfortable realities from the manifest destiny of dominant ideas. This has often been achieved as the basis of other works criticising the events of 1492. Columbus the vainglorious villain, the despoiler and destroyer, the imperialist *par excellence*, is not a latter-day discovery. He was recognised as such even by many of his contemporaries. His anti-eminence in the 1990s can be just another reformulation, just as much implicated in the events of 1492, just another angled perspective of *oculus mundi*.

It appears that the same subtle manipulation of knowledge and ignorance is at work in the quincentennial as in the heady days of Columbus. The encounter with reality – and even more important, with the Other – is still waiting to take place. We can break out of this vicious circle and liberate political debate only by healing the blindness that struck the eye of Europe and crippled its vision. This we must do by recognising the falsity of the invented Other and by consigning everything built on this mythology to the dustbin of history.

In this gigantic and vast re-making of a New World, the Others, as real peoples of the not-West, have a major role. They alone can offer the world the mental tools with which to cut through the intellectual and cultural rubbish of the past accumulated within the present. It is their experience of wrestling with their own ambiguous identity that contains the kernels of resistance and defiance on which a genuine plural future can be created. The powerful seldom contemplate sharing their world with the powerless – until the case for change has become an unavoidable practical necessity. What is required, therefore, in addition to a moral case is a practical framework on which to promote actual change.

The not-West must learn to talk to itself and of itself through its own language, so as to initiate a contemporary, unapologetic discourse concerning itself, unmediated thought the concepts imbibed in the epoch of Christopher Columbus. This involves re-learning the flexibility and dynamics of its own traditions and history. Only when its through and debate are grounded in its own conceptual universe can it hope to create a new relationship with the Western world and author its own post-modern reality. This new discourse may require a fresh definition of our institutions, especially in the area of knowledge generation and transmission. Resistance and defiance may involve recasting the educational structures of the Third World, building new intellectual networks that interrelate the South. These structures must revive a plethora of languages outside the Western imperium, each with its own vocabularies and concepts. Since they will all be informed by a common, though diverse, inheritance of dislocation and domination, they must come together to make multiple cultural discourses a reality, to establish a new plural future through cross-culture polylogue.

Such a polylogue may even help the modern West to encounter its own self without the distorting mediation of the reductionist Other. This is not a demand for effusion of guilt or for spectacular remorse but an acknowledgement that restitution and reparation, in addition to being a moral duty, can also be a prescription for inner health. The West's encounter with its real self is simultaneously a project for substantive change in the use of power in the

real world. The perpetual self-doubt that has often under-
lain the arrogance and presumptuousness of the West may
have to accommodate an awareness that differences by
themselves will not destabilise the Western self. The
existence of self-confident non-Western civilisations – even
when their categories are inaccessible and their values
remain incomprehensible to the West – does not presume
the negation of authentic Western identity.

To make such self-confidence viable, a discourse of new
ideas, and a sharp break from modernity and post-
modernity, has to be constructed to make the previously
disenfranchised world intelligible to the West and the West
intelligible to the rest of the world as a subdominant
presence.

This may mean overturning the pervasive reliance on the
concepts and images of newness, rupture and discontinuity
that have falsified the West to itself. It may also involve,
first, learning to appreciate the vital integrity of cultures
and civilisations as ongoing entities, bodies of interrelated
beliefs, values and practices that are meaningless except as
coherent wholes; and, second, appreciating that a multi-
civilisational future is not a recipe for conflict, mutual
incomprehensibility or chaos, but the means to a new
multiverse of possibilities, to a more sustainable and just
future, in social, political, economic and environmental
terms.

The challenge in the 1990s and hereafter must be to
recover our plural pasts, and, through them, our plural
futures so that once again there can begin to be histories,
metahistories and mythographies as various and equally
valid ways of seeing the world and constructing the past,
and as equally valid responses to events and ideas that

sustain a plural future for the world's peoples in all their diversity. This is the only means by which the debates silenced by Columbus's success may be reclaimed.

Select Bibliography

Arens, William, *The Man Eating Myth*, Oxford University Press, Oxford, 1979.

Asad, Talal, *Anthropology and the Colonial Encounter*, Ithaca Press, London, 1973.

Axtell, James, *The European and the Indian: Essays in the Ethnohistory of Colonial North America*, Oxford University Press, Oxford and New York, 1981.

Boxer, C. R, *The Portuguese Seaborne Empire 1415-1825*, Carcenet, London, 1991.

Columbus, Christopher, *The Four Voyages*, Penguin, Harmondsworth, 1969.

Daniel, Norman, *Heroes and Saracens*, Edinburgh University Press, Edinburgh, 1984.

—— *Islam, Europe and Empire*, Edinburgh University Press, Edinburgh, 1967.

Davies, Merryl Wyn, *Knowing One another: Shaping an Islamic Anthropology*, Mansell, London, 1988.

Fernandez-Armesto, Felipe, *Before Columbus: Exploration and Colonisation from the Mediterranean to the Atlantic 1229-1492*, Macmillan, London, 1987.

—— *Columbus*, Oxford University Press, Oxford, 1991.

Findley, M. I., *The Use and Abuse of History*, Hogarth Press, London, 1986.

Gabriel, Ralph Henry, *The Lure of the Frontier: A Story of Race Conflict*, Yale University Press, New Haven, 1929.

Hale J. R., *Rennaissance Europe 1480-1520*. Fontana, London, 1971.

Hartog, F., *Le Miroir d'Herodote: Eassai sur la representation de l'autre*, Gallimard, Paris, 1980.

Hemming, John, *Red Gold: The Conquest of the Brazilian Indians,* Macmillan, London, 1978.

Hodgen, Margaret T., *Early Anthropology in the Sixteenth and Seventeenth Centuries,* University of Pennsylvania Press, Philadelphia, 1964.

Jefferson, Thomas, *Notes on the States of Virginia,* ed. William Peyden, University of North Carolina Press, Chapel Hill, 1987.

Johnson, Paul, *A History of Christianity,* Penguin, Harmondsworth, 1978.

Kirkpatrick Sale, *The Conquest of Paradise,* Hodder and Stoughton, London, 1990.

Koning, Hans, *Columbus: His Enterprise,* Latin American Bureau, London, 1991.

Maalouf, Amin, *The Crusades Through Arab Eyes,* Al Saqi Books, London, 1984.

Mason, Peter, *Deconstructing America: Representations of the Other,* Routledge, London, 1990.

Nandy, Ashis, *The Intimate Enemy: The Loss and Recovery of Self Under Colonialism,* Oxford University Press, Oxford and Delhi, 1983.

—— *Traditions, Tyranny and Utopias: Essays in Politics of Awareness,* Oxford University Press, Oxford and Delhi, 1987.

Newitt, Malyn, *The First Portuguese Empire,* University of Exeter, Exeter, 1986.

Padgen, Anthony, *European Encounter with the New World,* Yale University Press, New Haven, 1993.

—— *Spanish Imperialism and the Political Imagination,* Yale University Press, New Haven, 1990.

—— *The Fall of the Natural Man,* Cambridge University Press, Cambridge, 1982.

Parry, J. H., *The Spanish Seaborne Empire,* University of California Press, Berkeley, 1966.

Phillips, J. R. S., *The Medieval Expansion of Europe,* Oxford University Press, Oxford, 1988.

Runciman, Steven, *A History of the Crusades*, (three vols.), Penguin, Harmondsworth, 1965.

Sardar, Ziauddin and Davies, Merryl Wyn, *Distorted Imagination: Lessons from the Rushdie Affair*, Grey Seal, London, 1990.

Slotkin, J. S., *Readings in Early Anthropology*, Aldine, Chicago, 1965.

Southern, R. W., *The Making of the Middle Ages*, Hutchinson, London, 1967.

—— *Western Society and the Church in the Middle Ages*, Penguin, Harmondsworth, 1970.

Stocking, G. Jr., *Race, Culture and Evolution: Essays in the History of Anthropology*, University of Chicago Press, Chicago, 1982.

Thomas, Keith, *Man and the Natural World*, Penguin, Harmondsworth, 1984.

—— *Religion and the Decline of Magic*, Penguin, Harmondsworth, 1973.

Welsh, Herbert, *The Indian Question: Past and Present*, Philadelphia, 1890.

Williams, Gwyn A., *Madoc: The Making of a Myth*, Eyre Methuen, London, 1979.

Wolf, Eric R., *Europe and the People Without History*, California University Press, Berkeley, 1982.